God Bothering

Our Journey Away from God

Stuart Abercrombie & Malcolm Hobbs

authorHOUSE®

AuthorHouse™ UK Ltd.
500 Avebury Boulevard
Central Milton Keynes, MK9 2BE
www.authorhouse.co.uk
Phone: 08001974150

First published by AuthorHouse 1/27/2010

ISBN: 978-1-4490-6296-5 (sc)

This book is printed on acid-free paper.

Contents

Introduction

If you live in England, the chances are you've probably seen the Alpha Course slogan somewhere. On billboards, in cinema adverts and in viral Internet videos, it asks, "Is There More To Life Than This?" The Alpha answer involves Bible reading and prayer, avoiding premarital sex and horoscopes, battling demonic activity, and speaking in a mysterious incomprehensible language.

Given this, you might be surprised to learn that the Alpha Course is the most popular Christian course in the UK today. In 2005 there were 7215 British churches registered as running the course, as well as hundreds of other institutions. Abroad, there were a further 16,000 churches running it. All of these efforts are supported by a stream of publications and promotions from Holy Trinity Brompton, the wealthy London church where Alpha started. Dozens of conferences run each year to train advisers, and there is now a theological college, St Paul's Theological Centre, dedicated to Alpha ideology.[1] The course is available in forms tailored to children, students, pensioners, military personnel, and prisoners. For all these people it claims to offer an opportunity to "explore the meaning of life". Over ten "thought-provoking weekly sessions" and a special Holy Spirit weekend event, a particular brand of Christianity is presented as the missing ingredient of a soulless 21st century life.[2]

Perhaps Alpha's most prominent convert is the disgraced cabinet minister, Jonathan Aitken, who was sustained through a perjury stretch by renewed Christian faith after a timely Alpha-instigated meeting with the Holy Spirit in a Worthing hotel. He revealed this during a talk he gave at my local church. The talk was heavy on inspiring redemption, less so on the still unresolved allegations of pimping and arms dealing that ultimately led to his imprisonment. Aitken prefers to talk of other things, in particular Alpha. In his book, *Heroes and Contemporaries*, he describes the man who runs the Alpha course, Nicky Gumbel, as "the world's most successful Christian evangelist of the twenty-first century". As justification he points to the "1 million a year rate of individuals doing Alpha courses".[3]

We take Alpha to be representative of Christianity today – the growing, Evangelical part. It is true that new courses have appeared, and Alpha's growth in British churches might have plateaued,[4] but Alpha continues to expand into new areas, particularly abroad. It is still seen as one of the most effective forms of Christian evangelism in Britain today, and rival courses owe much to it.

Given Alpha's power and success, we decided to test it. We would see only one form of Christianity, but we would see the story presented whole: everything that has convinced so many others would be there, ready to persuade. While we did not begin the course as committed Christians, that could not be necessary to take the measure of Alpha, otherwise the course could not achieve its stated goals. A visit to any Christian bookshop will show how often the story is told of people turning to Christianity after wasted years, whether originally atheistic or indifferent or pledged to another faith. This book records our efforts to experience something similar under the guidance of Alpha. We do not have theological qualifications, but nor do most of Alpha's converts, and nor do those thousands of other people whose conversion stories are taken to be so meaningful.

This is a personal account, based on our experiences with one course (it is written from S.A.'s point of view). It is an attempt to understand modern techniques used to spread Christianity, not a systematic analysis of the Bible. However, it is not possible to critically evaluate the Alpha Course without confronting basic questions about Christianity. We are not setting out to prove that God doesn't exist, and this is not about whether religion in general is a good or a bad thing; it's about whether what the Alpha course tells us is believable, and how it plays with the people who go there to learn about what its promoters call "basic Christianity".[5] But much of what we discuss does relate to Evangelical Christianity in general because the same core arguments tend to be repeated.

It also bears on the debate around the "new atheists". In response to Dawkins, Grayling, et al. some people say they caricature religious people – that they argue against a lunatic fringe and then load that criticism onto ordinary, reasonable believers in their bid to discredit all religion. Most religious types, we are told, are just nice people who yearn for something beyond barren materialism.

Take John Humphrys, for instance. In the *Sunday Times*[6] he reported his findings from "putting [his] fingers on the religious pulse of the nation". Amid anti-atheist clichés (e.g. "[c]ount the number of atheists in the foxholes") he made the point that not all believers are fundamentalist zealots. He cited conversations with the liberal theologian, Giles Fraser, who isn't sure if Jesus was resurrected, and who believes that "[e]vangelicals have misunderstood the Bible". "What's interesting," Humphrys declared, "is that you get much the same answer [to the question of why Christians believe] whether it comes from… Giles Fraser or… Rowan Williams or an old lady who has never read a book on theology in her life…"

Humphrys's case is founded on a particular vision of benign, undogmatic belief that does not ultimately claim to be based on empirical evidence or rational analysis. But the image that he and similar writers present is deeply inaccurate when considering the fastest growing and loudest churches in Britain, let alone anywhere else. Old-fashioned church fete Christianity is dying off with its elderly parishioners and is being replaced by a Christianity of a very different type, broadly known as Evangelical Christianity. Many Evangelicals today would not even admit the charming Rev Fraser was a Christian. They believe Rowan Williams isn't fit to lead the Anglican Church. They don't like gays; they watch for demonic activity; and they don't view the two as unconnected. They say their faith stems from incontrovertible evidence and imposes incontrovertible moral laws. As we show, Alpha, based in the Church of England, is part of and promotes this trend.

Contrary to Humphrys et al., what can be proven through evidence and logic *is* a crucial part of religious debate, even in the Church of England, and it is growing in importance. Certainly it is central to Alpha. Whether or not faith, in some harmless form, lends "meaning" to people's lives, the arguments used to promote its Evangelical variant are astonishingly vague and the evidence is thin to non-existent. Yet there are crowds of enthusiastic followers forcefully saying otherwise, all over the country and the world. This is our attempt to counterbalance in some small way the thousands of Evangelical Christian books currently in print. Our journey did not lead to the Alpha life, and we feel it is worth explaining why.

Notes

1. Figures from Booker, M. & Ireland, M. (2005). *Evangelism – Which way now?* (2nd Ed). Church House Publishing, p 12.
2. http://www.alpha.org, accessed Aug 2007.
3. Aitken, J. (2006). *Heroes and Contemporaries.* Continuum, p.223.
4. *Evangelism – Which way now?* p.14.
5. http://www.alphaph.org/organisation/origins. Accessed Dec 2008.
6. "In God We doubt", *Sunday Times,* September 2nd 2007.

A Note on the Text

The names of all the attendees and organizers of the Alpha Course we attended have been altered to safeguard their privacy. All biblical quotations are from New International Version unless otherwise noted. References to the background essays in *The New Oxford Annotated Bible*, third edition, OUP, 2001 are given with the abbreviation *TNOAB* and a page number.

We quote from a number of Alpha texts in the book, all written by Nicky Gumbel. Their details are given below. In the text only the titles and page numbers are given.

Questions of Life, Kingsway Communications, 2004: The main course text, closely following the content of the talks.

Searching Issues, Kingsway Communications, 2003: Designed to address the "seven most common questions raised on the Alpha Course", this is intended for post-Alpha study.

How to Run the Alpha Course, Kingsway Communications, 2004: This combines inspiring testimony from attendees with some instruction for course leaders and helpers.

30 Days, Alpha Publications, 2001: Billed as a "practical introduction to reading the Bible", this discusses thirty assorted biblical passages.

The Da Vinci Code: a response, Alpha International, 2006: Gumbel's attack on claims regarding Jesus associated with the novel *The Da Vinci Code* by Dan Brown.

Challenging Lifestyle, Kingsway Communications, 2004: Billed as "an official follow-up to the Alpha Course", this is an examination of the version of the Sermon on the Mount found in Matthew's Gospel.

A Life Worth Living, Kingsway Communications, 2004: Another follow-up to the Alpha course, this time based on Paul's epistle to the Philippians.

We would like the thank Ian, Helen, Nikki and Matthew for their useful comments and support in writing this book. Cover design courtesy of Studio Columba.

PROLOGUE

Nadi International Airport, Fiji

The immigration official with the outsized aviators flicked disdainfully through my passport. "Onward ticket please", I didn't have one – not a surprise, since I'd never intended to visit Fiji. I'd been cajoled, without proper documentation, onto a plane from Vanuatu on account of a visa problem. I tried to explain to the official. I said the airline could confirm my story, but they had gone home for the night and I couldn't produce proof of the ticket I needed to enter the country.

Before I knew it I was sitting on a bench with a Fijian string band playing "You Are My Sunshine" in the background. Not sure what to do with me, the Fijians shuffled papers for a few hours before an official came back with some documents. He made me repeat my story, and at the end let out a heavy sigh, massaged his forehead and said, "Why do they keep doing this to us? We cannot let you into Fiji without an onward ticket. You will be sent back to Port Vila. It is their job to sort you out, not ours. There is a flight on Thursday. Until then you will be put in a hotel at the airline's expense, but your movements will be restricted."

A hotel at the airline's expense? If I made my connecting flight I would only have to be in the hotel a couple of days – that didn't seem so bad. I gladly allowed myself to be escorted to a waiting people carrier where two tall Fijian security guards, dressed in brightly coloured flowery shirts, greeted me.

"What's the name of the hotel?" I asked, once we were underway.

"The Hotel Kennedy. It has a swimming pool and is only 10 minutes away." The Hotel Kennedy…it wasn't the Hilton but had a nice ring to it – and a swimming pool. I would enjoy my brief stay in luxury.

I was in for a shock. Reception turned out to be someone sitting in a protective cage, rundown-US-whorehouse style. I noted the slip I signed said "detainee" not "guest". They checked that I didn't have a mobile phone and told me that I was not allowed any phone calls.

The Hotel Kennedy was a bizarre set-up: a backpacker hostel that doubled as a detention centre. For backpackers there were pool tables downstairs, the stagnant pond masquerading as a swimming pool, and fridges stacked with beer and soft drinks. However, one section had been converted to cells suitable for locking up detainees awaiting deportation. That was where I was staying.

The heavy door had several locks on it and a huge bolt that slid across from the outside, making a suitably prison-like screeching noise of metal on metal as it did so. There were bars and thick wire mesh over the window.

On the other hand, the room had its comforts. I had a double bed, a TV with one channel devoted to Bollywood films, a cheap painting depicting a charming European forest scene, an air conditioning unit that dripped condensation onto my pillow, and a Bible. There was even an en suite bathroom, although the water was off for 15 hours a day. As if to taunt the detainee they'd provided a glossy visitor's guide to Fiji, with pictures of happy tourists frolicking on tropical beaches.

Shortly after arrival they delivered my first meal to my room. It consisted of a half portion of salty rice, sparingly sprinkled with assorted vegetables and some nauseatingly sweet cordial. In fact all of the meals were like this with the exception of breakfast, which consisted of two slices of buttered bread cut into triangles and a foul spiced tea. The airline was only required to pay for the cheapest option and the meagre portions always left me hungry.

After the meal, I took stock of my situation. I could handle it, I decided. After all, I had all my possessions, including a laptop and a book, and there was the TV – I could surely last two nights of confinement. I screwed up the visitor's guide in disgust and tossed the Bible into the corner. I certainly wouldn't need that – I had an autobiography of David Attenborough to read.

My optimism didn't last, as matters soon deteriorated. First, the power went down on the second day, never to return. I lost lighting, air conditioning, TV and power for the laptop. The only entertainment this left was the biography and, lying in the corner, the Bible. I could read these during the daylight hours, which lasted until about 6pm. After that I could do nothing but lie in darkness until morning. Second, my guard, Johnny, offered to change any Australian currency and buy me goods from the local shop if I gave him the money. Prison exchange rates were atrocious and I was duly ripped off. I blew the little cash he returned to me on the only items he would get me: two overpriced beers and a packet of cigarettes. Then the manager told me that my flight out of Fiji had been cancelled.

"Cancelled!? So when am I leaving?"

"They did not say."

"Well, I need to speak to them. Let me use the phone!"

"You cannot use the phone. They can phone you but you cannot phone them."

"But I need to know when I'm leaving! I'll miss my connecting flight in Vanuatu and that means missing my flight home! I need to organize another flight to Australia. I must talk to them."

"You are not allowed phone calls."

"Well what about my embassy? No one knows I am here. I must be allowed to talk to my embassy surely, isn't it a basic human right?"

"No phone calls."

This carried on for some time. The hotel staff had no power to change anything and were just there to look after me. Eventually, the manager agreed to phone immigration and relay a request from me to purchase a ticket on the next flight to Australia. "No" was their reply, without explanation.

This was the point when real frustration and despair set in. I had no idea when I would be allowed to leave. I was about to miss all my connecting flights to Australia and beyond. Nobody knew I was here. I could not talk to anyone, even my embassy. But the maddening thing was not being able to even discuss the matter with the people who were deciding my fate. I was powerless.

I spent most of the afternoon pacing up and down the 4ft length of floor in my cell, feverishly running everything through my head. I knew exactly what a caged animal in the zoo feels like. The frustration was excruciating. I started devoting time to throwing my pillow round the room. And then there was a glimmer of hope as I heard English voices downstairs. There were English backpackers checking in.

As they walked up the stairs past my room I called out to them. They looked around in bewilderment at first. I blurted out my story as fast as I could. They were a young well-spoken couple from Surrey and were shocked at my story, gasping, "Oh my God! But isn't this a Commonwealth country?" whenever they could. They agreed to phone the British embassy and got out a pen and paper

At this point Johnny, having realized what was happening, was frantically trying to unlock my door. I finished giving all my details just as he entered the room, shaking his head. As I was escorted downstairs the British couple were coming back, explaining that the embassy was closed until Monday. Johnny stopped them and took all three of us to the dining area. He gave them a stern lecture that they were not to talk to or help me. I then had to sit with him for three hours to make sure I didn't talk to anyone else. At this point I exploded. I had been calm around the staff up until this point but now I let it all out. I thumped the table a lot, cursed Fiji endlessly and shouted obscenities. Johnny just sat back – he'd seen it all before. Once I had stopped shouting he sat and quietly tried to reassure me. I would "just have to wait," he said.

The next few days were torturous. The staff expressed dismay, telling me most people only stayed a day or two. But then they mentioned odd cases when detainees had been there for several months. I was permanently slightly hungry. I was sick of the freezing water and the stuffy room. I had finished Attenborough and I had nothing left to occupy myself. I was alone 22 hours a day in my cell with nothing to do. I often found it difficult to sit still and would pace endlessly. I would do anything to try to pass the time. I spent hours drawing elaborate pictures on any scrap paper I could find, and taking pictures of nothingness with my camera round the room. I lay there after dark alone with my thoughts, fruitlessly willing sleep.

It must have been the Saturday when I was lying listlessly on my bed. There had been no word from immigration for days and I had just missed my connecting flight to Australia, and thus it seemed my flight back to the UK. I was feeling utterly dejected, hungry, stiff and hollow-eyed from being cooped up in this cell. I was not due back home for a long while yet, so no one would realize I might be in trouble. I felt abandoned by the world. Out the corner of my eye I spied the Bible, untouched since the first day. I picked it up. Was there really no one I could turn to…?

CHAPTER 1

A Jesus-Shaped Hole

The first step in an Alpha Course is usually the Alpha Supper. Titled in the past "Christianity: Boring, Untrue and Irrelevant?", it is now called "Is there more to life than this?" The food is heavily advertised, as is the "no pressure" approach: "just come along and find out what it's like!"

My course was at a local church whose nondescript aspect belied the shining, upholstered interior. It was not a draughty stone hall with hard pews, but a carpeted, brightly lit, friendly-looking place outfitted with the latest audio-visual equipment. Spread through the church were around twenty tables, all with neatly laid places with napkins and wine.

Solitary thought was not encouraged. As soon as I entered I was jumped by a smiley woman with earrings made from feathers, who immediately began vigorously questioning me about anything she could think of, making sure along the way to learn my past church attendance record. Noticing my failure to mingle, she called in the large, leather-jacketed George, a church stalwart (although he later told me he'd been voted off the parish council by "old fogeys"), and a young-but-greying patent attorney called Oscar, who'd just begun his association with the church. From the stickers we all had to wear I found the woman's name was Celia.

"I'm a dangerous man," George soon told me. "They say a little knowledge is a dangerous thing – I know a little about everything!"

The hot topic was Sunday's Jonathan Aitken talk. Celia had been there but claimed not to remember any details, and kept prompting me to remember Aitken's hilarious prison rhyming slang. I didn't fully cooperate, but George was happy to fill in for any conversational slackers. Aitken, we were soon airily informed, was almost certainly innocent. Yes he'd made a mistake with the libel case and had been caught out, but those papers were after him from the beginning. Pretty much anybody would have done what he'd done given the unholy pressure he was under from the "Manchester Guardian".

"But what about these allegations of smoothing the way for corrupt arms deals, and procuring…" I asked. I didn't feel comfortable raising this element of the scandal.

"Girls," Celia helpfully supplied.

"Oh, I'm 95% sure he didn't do any of that", averred George. "And who knows what goes on with these deals? It's all part of being a government minister. But the newspapers – they jump on anything. Just because of this hotel bill…"

I checked later and found the Ritz hotel bill was crucial because Aitken was alleged to have met a Saudi business partner, Said Ayas, there to arrange arms deals between UK firms and Ayas's boss, Prince Mohammed – the son of the Saudi king. The fact that the bill wasn't paid by his wife, as he claimed, was suggestive of a bigger story.[1] But I didn't have the details of the Aitken allegations to hand. "So you don't think there was corruption then?"

"These newspapers will get you on anything," George thundered on. So I left it, and soon we sat down. The only interlude came when a large Alpha alumna was brought out on stage to tell us how last year's course had changed her life. The fulcrum moment had been what she called "the Saturday" – the weekend session where the Holy Spirit is called down and people speak in tongues.

Once seated, George's new concern was the male-dominated make-up of our table: we only had Celia to share between four men, and therefore had to locate "some crumpet". After a long search all he could turn up was a heavily pregnant woman and her husband. Still, it was a fresh audience, and George took advantage of it. In the background I could hear him still talking about "that silly hotel bill" as Celia recounted, almost with relish, how the two previous vicars had been affected by tragic deaths. It was all OK, it turned out, because they attended such a supportive church.

The conversation took in patent law, although the main topic was the death of Ronnie Barker, and the sad state of comedy today.

Modern comedians are too rude, the table agreed – nothing like the Two Ronnies. Oscar the patent attorney contributed a story from the radio about a bleach spillage on the M25 near Staines. He strained for other humorous spillages. Eventually one came: a spillage of "respect" near Diss. Mirth ensued.

All through was the frequent emphasis from George and Celia, and the curate afterwards, that the course carried no obligation – none at all. Absolutely none. People can leave whenever they like. Some people leave after the first week, others after a few weeks; but because the course is so well done many choose to stay. And that's fine too. Other than this, and passing round a list for those interested in the course proper, there was no talk of the course itself (except an avowal from George that it had been uniformly misrepresented by the demonic newspapers) or Christianity. There seemed to be a deliberate effort to steer clear of religiosity, and instead to show how normal they all were.

At one point George took a moment out from newspaper bashing to relay a computing nugget he'd remembered: the story of how the term "bug" arose.

"Yes, I've heard the story…"

"They say it was with the early computers…"

"An insect…"

"Apparently it was a moth in one of the relays," he ploughed on.

"Right. I heard that theory…"

"Bryson mentions it I think – in one of these huge old machines…"

"I think perhaps it's apocryphal, but maybe it's true."

"Oh."

And then we were on to the introductory film, where Nicky Gumbel, the figurehead and chief author of the Alpha Course, explained that falling church attendance was a terrible thing, because so many of us have a Jesus-shaped hole in our lives. Tragically for *Private Eye*'s credibility, he used one of their "humorous" Christianity pieces, about God leaving the Church of England, to illustrate his point. It was a standard issue Anglican sermon that compared a life without Christ to watching TV with a broken aerial. No direct facts were presented to justify Christian belief, even though the talk's title was "Christianity:

Boring, Untrue or Irrelevant?" Instead, examples of intelligent believers – Isaac Newton[2] and Thomas Arnold and so on – were produced, alongside a long stream of tangentially relevant humorous anecdotes. All the way through, George guffawed and turned to check that I was sharing the fun.

Gumbel comes over as the Tony Blair of Christianity – a plausible, friendly kind of chap, who nonetheless always seems to skirt the main issue. He has a high-pitched, singsong voice, but a steely grey Clooney aspect. I immediately assumed he was a hit with certain female parishioners. A sociological study called *Anyone for Alpha* provided confirmation:

"At one church that ran *Alpha*, so I discovered, a number of ladies ranging from 50 to 80 years old only attended because they wanted to see Gumbel. Each week they would huddle excitedly around the television set to see the main attraction. One of them made a special visit to HTB [Holy Trinity Brompton] just to see Gumbel personally. It was, she claimed, one of the best days of her life! Such is the impact of *Alpha*."[3]

About the only notable content was on the difference between "intellectual" and "personal" knowledge: a distinction between book learning and feeling, as far as I could see. This seemed an attempt to de-emphasize historical evidence in favour of personal experiences with the Holy Spirit, although Gumbel elsewhere does promote appealing both to the "mind" and the "heart", to allow a "faith based on reasonable grounds" rather than a "'blind leap' of faith".[4]

With the film finished and some weirdly earnest goodbyes, we were off into the night. I didn't feel I'd learnt anything, let alone tackled whether Christianity was boring or untrue or irrelevant. We'd had a standard "life is empty without Christ" sales pitch, and Gumbel had strenuously tried to be funny, but it hardly seemed designed to draw in anyone who had previously thought much about whether Christianity was untrue.

It seemed to me that if Christianity was untrue it was almost certainly, if not irrelevant, then at least less relevant than commonly supposed. But we hadn't covered its truth directly at all. All we could come away with was a vague feeling that it worked for some people, so perhaps it might work for us.

Notes

1. "Aitken, the fixer and the secret multi-million pound arms deals", *Guardian*, 5th March 1999.
2. Gumbel also emphasizes Isaac Newton's Christian faith in *Searching Issues* (p.88). Omitted is the fact that Isaac Newton was not an orthodox Christian at all, according to Gumbel's standards, as he did not believe in the Trinity.
3. Hunt, S. (2001). *Anyone for Alpha?* Darton, Longman and Todd Ltd., p.43.
4. *How to Run the Alpha Course*, p.36.

CHAPTER 2

Irresistibly Attractive as a Man

As far as I was concerned, this was the one on which it all stood or fell. In the session after the previous week's "supper" we were promised an answer to the question, "Who Was Jesus?" In a course that claimed to reveal the meaning of life this had to be the key, because the answers all rested on belief in Jesus as the Son of God. After the tantalising video the previous week, how could anybody not want to evaluate Jesus's credentials? The strange thing was, nobody else seemed to agree that this was the hinge on which the course turned.

First there was the inevitable meal and talk to get through. The welcome seemed cooler than the previous week, although nobody made it through the door without being assigned a name badge. Celia said hello, but George was too busy declaiming to somebody else to turn in my direction. It turned out that my mentors had been reassigned. Soon after we sat down to eat, central command dispatched fellow group member Anne to introduce herself. A young, chatty woman, her main focus in life aside from teacher training seemed to be Alpha. In fact she had been to three Alpha Courses. Was it possible to learn any more? She giggled and made an admission: she was a plant!

Although she said she wasn't supposed to reveal it, she admitted she was a covert "helper". Her job was to participate in our group in the guise of a disinterested party, and to help the discussion along in the right direction, but to be "less intimidating" than the official Leader. Sure enough, when it came to the group introductions her quasi-official status wasn't mentioned. I later learned that these helpers are standard in Alpha groups. It became more obvious why the group structure was so rigid. Coloured dots on the name badges had been carefully distributed to ensure the right group mix, and if my friend Malc hadn't unexpectedly come along this week my group would have had a majority of people already committed to the Alpha way. As it was, wavering Christians just about predominated. Every group had its own room because there was a tendency "to get emotional". Our emotions were to be confined to the vestry.

The talk, delivered in chatty style by the local university chaplain, Tom, followed Gumbel's script in *Questions of Life* closely. We were, Tom stressed, "drowning" in evidence for Jesus. He reeled off a few names of ancient historians – Josephus, Tacitus, Suetonius. Then he talked at length about how the Bible texts had not been corrupted after their authors wrote them. Because there are so many New Testament manuscripts from a few centuries after Jesus, we can trust that the texts we have now are fairly close to what Matthew, Mark, Luke and John wrote. He did not, however, address whether these accounts were truthful or well-informed.

Having established the Gospels' credentials in the space of ten minutes, we skipped to a moral case for Jesus as God. There were three explanations for Jesus's outrageous hints that he was God: that he was mad, evil or telling the truth. This is the old "trilemma" argument from C.S.Lewis, whom Gumbel approvingly quotes. The full version of the quoted passage reads:

'I am trying here to prevent anyone saying the really foolish thing that people often say about Him: "I'm ready to accept Jesus as a great moral teacher, but I don't accept His claim to be God." That is the one thing we must not say. A man who was merely a man and said the sort of things Jesus said would not be a great moral teacher. He would either be a lunatic – on a level with the man who says he is a poached egg – or else he would be the Devil of Hell. You must make your choice. Either this man was, and is, the Son of God: or else a madman or something worse. You can shut Him up for a fool, you can spit at Him and kill Him as a demon; or you can fall at His feet and call Him Lord and God. But let us not come with any patronising nonsense about His being a great human teacher. He has not left that open to us. He did not intend to.'[1]

He couldn't be mad or lying because his moral teachings were uniquely wonderful and had never been improved upon. "The teaching of Jesus is widely acknowledged to be the greatest teaching that has ever fallen from human lips," declares Gumbel. "[I]n nearly 2,000 years no one has improved on the moral teaching of Jesus Christ. Could that teaching really have come from someone evil or insane?"[2] This argument is a great favourite of Christians, and yet it spurs all sorts of questions that, to my knowledge, have never been answered.

The "greatest teaching" claim surely presupposes a pro-Christian bias: no Muslim would accept that Jesus's moral teachings were unsurpassed. To take Jesus's unparalleled standing as a teacher on trust, as "widely acknowledged", is to take a significant step towards the Christian faith without supplying any justification.

In any case, what in the Bible justifies the great claim of moral uniqueness? Were Jesus's ideas genuinely radical? Not if we consider his summary of how to treat fellow human beings. His primary moral teaching was by his own admission just a distillation of the Jewish Ten Commandments. Regarding the so-called "Golden Rule" he said:

"So in everything, do to others what you would have them do to you, for this sums up the Law and the Prophets." (Matthew 7:12)

The Law and prophets were Jewish, and this is a reference to the Old Testament's Leviticus 19:18 – part of the Jewish Torah:

"Do not seek revenge or bear a grudge against one of your people, but love your neighbour as yourself. I am the Lord."

Gumbel is aware that the central principle of Jesus's ethics had been around centuries before him, and not just in the Bible. He admits this in *Searching Issues*, saying "it is not surprising that the essence of the 'golden rule'… is contained in almost every religion from Confucius (551-479 BC) onwards".[3] His explanation is that human beings are "in the image of God and God has given us a conscience with which to distinguish right and wrong." But if Jesus's moral teaching was embedded in everyone, even those before Jesus's time, what claim does he have to moral innovation? How is his rehash of a common moral principle extraordinary enough to confer divine status?

Even if the biblical Golden Rule were unique, it has long been known that it cannot be the ultimate ethical principle. The biblical "positive" version (it tells one what to *do* rather than what *not to do*), far from being obviously superior, as apologists sometimes suggest, is vulnerable to counter-examples that don't affect the "negative" Confucian formulation. For instance, a masochist is encouraged by Jesus's moral pronouncement to inflict pain on others. The rule, far from bringing otherworldly moral clarity, appears as fallible as other moral axioms produced by humans. For this reason various refinements have been proposed since his time.[4]

Gumbel never explicitly reveals the moral criteria that inform his decision to accept Jesus as God, so it is impossible to know if they are reasonable. Gautama Buddha is "widely acknowledged" to have espoused remarkable moral teachings, but Gumbel does not credit his religious claims. Was he a "madman or something worse"? Perhaps, because he never claimed to be God, he wasn't on a par with a self-proclaimed poached egg. But he was, one assumes, deluded or evil given the claims he made for his religious teaching, and yet he promoted a moral message that many find persuasive. If that is so, how reliable can the trilemma really be? "[W]e find good in many religions", says Gumbel elsewhere,[5] yet he fails to explore the implications for what he says is the basis for Christian belief. He ignores other religions in the Alpha Course itself, leaving followers further confusion if they ever pick up *Searching Issues*, where he still ultimately avoids the question.

If we follow the argument beyond *Questions of Life* we are left with a case based not on Jesus's unique morality but on the extremity of his reported claims – that unlike Buddha, etc. he supposedly said he was God, rather than just a teacher. This is all C.S.Lewis ultimately presents,[6] and it is obviously not rational. The grandness and improbability of a claim is not positively correlated with its truth; if anything the reverse is true. But even if this notion were accepted, its consistent application would hardly come to rest at Christianity given the catalogue of bizarre religious beliefs that have existed. The approach distinguishes Jesus from thousands of other god claimants only by implicitly ignoring them.

Alpha also implies that Jesus's personal moral *example*, rather than his teaching, singles him out as uniquely good. By way of evidence we hear only generalities about his miracles (turning water into wine showed he was a fun person[7]) and "love" (he sacrificed himself for us – another question-begging argument[8]), and plaudits from other fans. For instance Gumbel quotes former Lord Chancellor and reformed Hitler appeaser, Quintin Hogg, describing, presumably from personal revelation, why Jesus was "irresistibly attractive as a man":

"No pale Galilean he, but a veritable Pied Piper of Hamelin who would have the children laughing all round him and squealing with pleasure and joy as he picked them up."[9]

Whatever his abilities as a children's entertainer, Jesus delivered a message at odds with the loving Alpha image of him. He keenly reiterated the punishment in hell of those who didn't follow his teaching. Is it morally perfect to dispatch people who have never heard of Christianity to "everlasting fire"?[10] Or to categorically condemn those denying the Holy Spirit any chance of salvation?[11] It seems fair to assume a message of arbitrarily dispensed eternal damnation would not, in the end, lead to "squealing with pleasure and joy".

Nor can Gumbel easily detach Jesus from the moral message elsewhere in the Bible if he is to avoid abandoning standard Christian belief. For instance, Paul says in 1 Corinthians 14:34:

"Women should be silent in the churches. For they are not permitted to speak, but should be subordinate, as the law also says."

Just earlier, Anne and a rambling female student Alpha coordinator had both violated this sacred edict. Elsewhere, in 1 Corinthians 6:9, Paul includes perdition for homosexuals in the "unimprovable" Christian message – a passage that Gumbel cites against homosexuality.[12]

Paul was supposed to have interpreted Jesus's message in what we later learned was a "divinely-breathed" fashion. Christians hold him to be the most important mediator of Jesus's teachings who ever lived, without whose writings Christianity is unthinkable. As far as Gumbel is concerned, Paul's moral pronouncements were simply an expansion and explication of Jesus's. He must therefore view them as similarly perfect. But would most people agree that his anti-women, anti-gay stance had never been "improved on"?

An entirely different question turns on what Gumbel never spells out, but has to be assuming for his argument to work at all. He is implying that we can judge Jesus by some moral standard outside the Bible. In *Searching Issues* Gumbel says that in some sense humans are imprinted at birth with godly morality. Yet in *Questions of Life* he asserts that "[f]rom the Bible we know that certain things are wrong."[13] Which is it? If Christianity admits a morality not defined by the Bible then what is it and why do we need it mediated by the Bible? How can we resolve apparent contradictions between our imprinted moral sense and Christian texts? If there is no external standard – if morality really does stem only from the Bible – then no deduction about the Bible's truth can derive from it without the argument being circular: biblical morality cannot meaningfully be used to judge the goodness of biblical morality. If there is an answer, Gumbel does not give it; he would have to start by acknowledging the question.

The rest of the Alpha case is premised either on claims discussed above or aspects of Christianity not unique to that religion. We have Jesus's alleged fulfilment of Old Testament prophecy (see the next chapter) and his resurrection (but as usual we only have New Testament writers' word for this), and the "dramatic impact" of the rise of Christianity (but Islam expanded in an arguably more dramatic fashion). And we have the assertion that "[c]ountless of millions of people down the ages have experienced the risen Jesus Christ".[14] Given the number of people of other beliefs who claim to have "experienced" their incompatible gods, this is unconvincing, even before Gumbel vaunts the "common experience" Jesus's multifarious followers have had.

Firstly, their "common experience" only occurs – as far as it does occur – after they have been instructed in what experience to expect: people not exposed to Christianity have failed to experience the risen Jesus. Secondly, the multitude of Christian denominations strongly suggests that the experience is not that "common" after all. Presbyterian congregations, for instance, do not experience the gift of tongues that so excites Gumbel. Unitarians don't see Jesus as part of the Trinity. Jehovah's Witnesses don't even think he was crucified.[15] Going back to the very beginning of Christianity, we find other followers, dismissed as heretics today and persecuted in their time, who did not believe

Jesus was both a God and a man. The relative uniformity of Christian belief now is in part a result of a successful campaign to destroy rival interpretations[16] – hardly an advertisement for "common experience".

To summarize the Alpha message, Jesus was a uniquely good person, according to some vague and unstated standard, which means he must have been telling the truth when he said he was God. At least, he was said to have said he was God, and was said to have been good, disregarding his fixation with eternal torment and his association with the unsavoury ideas of Paul. We only have the New Testament writers' word for any of this, but then their work has been copied a lot, which means what they wrote hasn't been corrupted, which means that it must be true – when taken, that is, in tandem with scattered name-checks in a handful of non-biblical sources. We also have the claims of his numerous adherents, which are for some unexplained reason more credible than the claims of people following other religions. This, sadly, was as far as our understanding of the historical Jesus would go, for the following discussion would resolve nothing.

Notes

1. Lewis, C.S (2001). *Mere Christianity*. HarperCollins, p. 52.
2. *Questions of Life*, p.30.
3. *Searching Issues*, p.29.
4. One famous example is Kant's Categorical Imperative.
5. *Searching Issues*, p.30.
6. Lewis, C. S. (1979). What are we to make of Jesus Christ? In Hooper, W. (ed.) *God in the Dock: Essays in Theology and Ethics*. William B Eerdmans Publishing Co. Here Lewis explicitly compares Jesus with Buddha and Mohammed, saying his claims of divinity have "no parallel in other religions".
7. *Questions of Life*, p.31.
8. Ibid. He is saying we should believe that Jesus was the Son of God because he was uniquely good. A primary reason he gives for believing in this goodness is that Jesus sacrificed himself for us. The problem is that belief in this sacrifice assumes that Jesus was the Son of God, otherwise he was just another crucified man.
9. *Questions of Life*, p.32.
10. For the recurring motif of everlasting fire/punishment see Matthew 3:12, 8:18, 25:41, 25:46; Mark 9:42-43. In *Searching Issues* Gumbel claims the ignorant will not be punished. See below for discussion.
11. See Mark 3:29 and Matthew 12:31.

12. *Searching Issues*, p.72.
13. Questions of Life, p.102.
14. Questions of Life, p.36.
15. Evangelicals would tend to claim that the last two are not Christian at all, their reason being, fundamentally, that these people have *not* had a "common experience" of Jesus. This would obviously not help Gumbel's argument.
16. See Ehrman, B.D. (2005). *Lost Christianities: The Battles for Scripture and the Faiths We Never Knew*, OUP.

CHAPTER 3

What about Buddhism?

Of the two and a half hour evening of the first session, the discussion was allocated a little over half an hour, and first we had to introduce ourselves. Our Leader was Bill, a Scotsman with – he immediately told us – two theology degrees, who gave repeated grinning reassurances that scepticism was OK, as he'd once been a sceptic himself. His deputy Sandy was there as well, along with her husband Dr Phillip, and also the shill, Anne. There were two undecideds apart from us: Pete, a South African who professed to be "cynical", and a woman named Wilma, who had been coming to services for fifteen years, on and off, and didn't seem very clear why she was there.

"Are there any questions?" asked Bill. After two talks and two meals spanning many hours, stretched over two evenings, I felt we'd earned this moment.

Malc asked what Josephus, Tacitus and Suetonius had actually said, because it wasn't divulged in the talk. Bill gave no details, in spite of his extensive qualifications and former scepticism, but assured us the evidence was "good". Since he wasn't keen to contribute any hard information I threw in my recollections. An outline of what was said by these historians is given in Appendix A. The key points are:

a) The Josephus quotation supplied by Gumbel in his book is acknowledged by most scholars to have been altered by Christian forgers. The most glaring problem is that Josephus was a devout Jew, yet Gumbel quotes him declaring Jesus the Messiah.

b) Both Tacitus and Suetonius wrote around seventy years after

Jesus's death, and we have no reason to believe they were not simply passing on general gossip.

c) What these authors say is minimal. None of Jesus's life is described.

(Anne's answer to the objection about Josephus's faith was that "perhaps he was a… I can't remember their name… a sort of Jew who believed in Jesus". She apparently meant a "Messianic Jew", but we know that he was an observant Jew, quite possibly a Pharisee, so her answer is not persuasive.)

The weakness of these sources can be inferred from what Gumbel says they prove. He only says they show Jesus existed.[1] He cannot claim that they confirm the biblical picture of Jesus because even at face value they do not. At most they tell us that a religious leader named Jesus was executed by Pilate, and even this much is dubious (see Appendix A). Gumbel is apparently trading off familiarity with the Bible story to exaggerate what his evidence can support. Presumably this is why his book contains only a corrupted, hyperbolic statement from Josephus and nothing from Tacitus or Suetonius.

While some have argued Jesus was a mythical figure, rebutting that charge is far from establishing the Gospels as truthful. Apart from the Gospel authors, there is no one who reports any details of Jesus's birth, his healing miracles, his trial, his parables, or his resurrection.[2] Yet the occasional mention of his name in pagan sources dating from seventy years after his death is said to facilitate confident belief in these. Furthermore, Alpha is not just selling the idea that Jesus existed, or even that a resurrected miracle worker named Jesus existed, but a complete belief system based on claims made in the Old Testament, in books in the New Testament apart from the Gospels, and stemming from outside the Bible. The existence of Jesus says nothing about whether to believe the theology of Paul's epistles, let alone that adopted centuries after the Bible's authorship by the various church fathers and councils who defined and imposed orthodox Christianity.[3]

The Alpha syllabus didn't recognize any of this, and nor did the group. When I raised these concerns Bill merely shrugged. Although a key part of the talk had been on this historical evidence, on how compelling it was, the Leader and his deputies brushed off serious objections as "nitpicking" and "missing the big picture". The two waverers admitted they'd never considered these questions, but this didn't seem to worry them. The group flitted from thought to thought, without any strong interest in knowing if Jesus actually was the Son of God. It seemed an assumption they were prepared to make but not examine.

Bill's only answer, amid various fleeting contributions from others, was to amplify Gumbel's other argument by making the strange claim that Jesus is better attested to historically than Julius Caesar – a claim often heard from Evangelical apologists. This is only true according to a criterion that's impossible to justify: the number of early manuscripts referring to him. The argument runs that there are far more early copies of the New Testament than there are of, say, Julius Caesar's *Gallic War* or Tacitus's *Annals*. Whereas the biblical manuscripts date from a few hundred years after Jesus, the earliest copy of *Gallic War* is from almost a millennium after Caesar. A handy chart in *Questions of Life* emphasizes this.

Firstly, this argument undercuts the earlier idea that Tacitus et al. significantly corroborate the Bible in some way. If Tacitus's manuscripts are rare, and such rareness implies potential corruption and unreliability, then how much do they bolster Jesus's credentials? If, on the other hand, Gumbel is arguing that Tacitus et al. *and* the Bible are reliable, even though there are only around ten copies of *Annals*, then what does the relative profusion of biblical manuscripts tell us?

Secondly, the relative prevalence of Christian manuscripts is not surprising or unique. Religious texts are almost inevitably granted more diligent copying and preservation than other texts. That does not make them true. When considering the Muslim Quran or Hindu Vedas, Christians of course agree that popularity is no guide to truth; the Bible is the only religious text that receives their manuscript-counting treatment. This is understandable, because if we took the book enumeration path to historical truth seriously our picture of the ancient world would be a contradictory, cartoonish mess of gods and miracles, with no genuine history at all. We wouldn't just be more certain of Jesus than Julius Caesar; we'd view Mohammed's supernatural flight to Jerusalem as more likely than Caesar's crossing of the Rubicon.

Even if, as Gumbel and the group often tacitly assumed, Christianity were the only religion in existence, what could the number of early Bibles show? The earliest extant copies of the New Testament date from about three hundred years after Jesus's death. This confirms only that there wasn't wholesale modification of the New Testament from then on. It says nothing about the accuracy of what the Gospel authors originally wrote, or its possible modification in the centuries immediately following. This has to be considered because they made demonstrable historical errors in an apparent quest to fulfill prophecy (see later); they made frequent inherently implausible supernatural claims; and they wrote decades after Jesus's death and probably didn't have access to first-hand information. Nor do we know that the collection of books selected to form the New Testament presents an unbiased sampling of sources available at the time. None of this can be ignored because Gumbel's central "mad, bad or god" argument is founded on the unexamined assumption that the Gospel accounts are true and impartial.

As it happens, we have far better grounds to credit accounts of Julius Caesar. Bill asserted that the only historical text we have about him was his own *Gallic War*. This is false. Julius Caesar also wrote *Civil War*. Suetonius's *The Lives of the Caesars* has a chapter devoted to Julius Caesar, in contrast to the one or possibly two sentences mentioning Christians. We also have coins and inscriptions, as well as Tacitus, Cicero, Livy, Plutarch, Appian, Sallust, Nepos, Catullus and Dio Cassius, all of whom reveal far more biographical information about Caesar than the Gospels do about Jesus. In Cicero's letters we have a contemporary who knew Caesar, writing about himself and Caesar. There are multiple independent, detailed sources, including thousands of words by Julius Caesar himself. By contrast, we have nothing written by Jesus, and a selection of Gospels, three of which were based on one narrative account – that of Mark, about whom we know little except that he had a religion to push.[4] In summary, biblical textual corruption is a sideshow next to issues that Gumbel never addresses. There is a vast unbridged gap between "evidence for Jesus' existence" and the idea that supernatural conceptions of his life are "based on firm historical evidence".[5]

It hardly matters, given the central unaddressed issue of original Gospel truth, but Gumbel also ignores the divergence of biblical manuscripts. By the eighteenth century, thirty thousand textual variations had been uncovered. Today, hundreds of thousands of scribal slips and deliberate alterations are known, with a range of differing Greek manuscripts available to Bible translators. We have no idea exactly what the Gospel authors originally said, and the differences are not all trivial. We know, for instance, that Trinitarians managed to smuggle a passage affirming their belief into 1 John 5:7-8 – the so-called "Johannine comma" – something Gumbel knows about, but does not mention.[6] Various other changes are thought to have been made for doctrinal reasons, as well as by simple error.[7] Some of these changes are apparent from the textual evidence, and can be accounted for. But what else was modified in the centuries before the earliest manuscripts available today, during the battles between rival Christian factions? The victors had the means, and a strong motive, to alter what they have handed down to us. We know texts were altered and rival books destroyed. And yet apparently it is fine to take on trust what passed through their hands.

In response to these lines of argument, Bill reverted to the "leap of faith": "Your academic approach is fine, but in the end you've got to make a leap of faith." Evidence was not enough.

"But surely, if make a leap of faith you have to know it's the right one? I mean, plenty of people make a leap of faith but they end up with completely different beliefs. So don't you have to come back to the evidence to know?"

"Yes the evidence is important," replied Bill, and so we went round the circle again. The evidence was "firm", we'd been told, but in practice it wouldn't do to evaluate it too critically. The "leap of faith" would carry us over any gaps, but how we could know which leap to make – that was passed over in silence, or via deflections to other subjects.

Wilma was not interested in textual evidence. After a brief pause, she said, "I suppose it's because Christianity is peaceful."

"What about Buddhism?" I asked her.

She seemed taken aback. "I never thought about that. I suppose it's what we learn about in school…" She trailed off, apparently musing in silence. This was hardly the most important objection, because religions cannot be selected on these grounds; what matters is not how peaceful they are, but how true. But Wilma and the others were not concerned. For them belief seemed to be defined by comfort, not truth.

The group flitted to whether those who have never heard of Jesus can be saved. Bill followed the *Searching Issues* line that they can, in contravention of scripture.[8] It wasn't possible to question this properly because he soon worried aloud that our debate had become "a dialogue", with the others not contributing enough. I took the signal to shut up and listen as we meandered through various people's ideas about what would happen to unbelievers untouched by Jesus. Eventually, since it was at least supposed to be the point of the discussion, I felt obliged to raise again the content of the talk.

Gumbel holds that Jesus's fulfilment of prophecy is reason to believe he was God. He says Jesus bore out "over 300 prophecies" from the Old Testament.[9] *Questions of Life* cites three examples: the manner of Jesus's death and burial, and his place of birth. In the Alpha Bible reading course, *30 Days*, there is a fourth example, the virgin birth, omitted from main course book.[10] This last prophecy is discussed in chapter 7, but less significant ones give a picture.

Consider Matthew. In 2:23 he refers to "prophets" saying Jesus "will be called a Nazarene", but this prophecy appears nowhere in the Old Testament. In 3:3 he misquotes Isaiah 40:3 in order to fit it to John the Baptist's ministry. He goes on in the same vein, sometimes veering into comedy: 21:6-7 has Jesus riding two donkeys simultaneously, because Matthew didn't understand Zechariah 9:9 properly. He strains to fit his story to a tortured reading of Jewish messianic expectations and unrelated historical situations. Far from cementing Gospel credibility, supposedly fulfilled prophecies undermine it because the scenery keeps falling over.

The degree to which prophecy defined, rather than predicted, the Gospel accounts is illustrated by considering the circumstances of Jesus's birth. These are clearly a key part of any historical understanding of his life, and one of Gumbel's few specific prophetic claims is that Jesus's place of birth was predicted in Micah 5:2. (Matthew viewed this foreshadowing as remarkable enough to insert a misquotation of Micah into his Herod narrative.[11]) Plainly, Gumbel views the Gospel nativity accounts as important and credible. But how convincing are they?

They are not good on the date. Matthew says Jesus was born in the reign of Herod the Great,[12] who died in 4 BCE. He mentions no journey to Bethlehem, and implies Joseph and Mary were living there before Jesus's birth, only moving to Nazereth after Herod's death.[13] In Luke, by contrast, we find Joseph and Mary had left their home town of Nazereth for Bethlehem, on account of a Roman census conducted by the Roman governor of Syria, Quirinius.[14] The problem is that Quirinius only became governor in 6 CE. Luke says this was the first such census, and Josephus confirms that the first census was in 6 CE. There is a ten year gulf between the Matthew and Luke birth dates. Meanwhile, Matthew has Herod slaughtering infants[15] in an incident not mentioned anywhere else, in spite of Josephus's keen recording of his crimes, and the outcry it would have caused. He manages to work in an otherwise unmentioned flight to Egypt, which allows him to cite a totally unrelated passage in Hosea 11:1 as yet another fulfilled prophecy.[16]

All of this might seem trivial, and it is to somebody prepared to accept that the Gospels are on occasion wrong, but apparently Gumbel is not one of those people. He believes that drawing attention to these clunking efforts will reinforce belief in Jesus when, to anyone prepared to countenance biblical fallibility, they point to a more plausible explanation: the authors bent the truth, and what they wrote is at least partly religious mythology, not history. If Jesus really had been born in Bethlehem, and fulfilled Micah 5:2 (leaving aside the separate issue of whether Micah 5:2 actually predicted what Matthew says it did), and the story had been reliably passed on to the authors, then we would not now have two contradictory Gospels with entirely different takes on how this happened. The same applies to numerous other details in the Gospels, all of which Gumbel takes as absolutely true. If even one of these is wrong, where does that leave the breather of scripture? Why did God mislead us? What can we trust in his book?

In the light of this unreliability, I asked Bill if we could be sure of anything about Jesus's birth – in particular whether his mother was a virgin.

"You don't have to believe in the Virgin Birth to be a Christian," he replied sharply, and rather misleadingly (see chapter 7).

"Well, OK, what about the resurrection? The Gospels have a lot of differences on that – different timing, different people at the tomb seeing different things. How can we be sure about these accounts?"

To take just one example, in the first three Gospels the Last Supper is a Passover meal.[17] In John 13:1 it happens "before the festival of Passover",[18] and a string of other verses after the Last Supper has Passover still in preparation (18:28, 19:14, 19:31).[19]

"It can look like that, but I think you'll find if you look into it they're actually very accurate. They don't actually contradict each other."

This view is common in fundamentalist apologetics,[20] and it is impossible to take seriously. Even if the accounts of Jesus's life could logically be reconciled, doing so relies on assuming the various writers arbitrarily decided to omit key details (like the presence of an angel in the tomb), used unheard of linguistic constructions, operated with an eccentric conception of time, assumed Jewish Law at variance with all other known sources, and so on. If we were at this stage evaluating the Bible as a credible source for miraculous events upon which Christian faith is based, didn't the need for such contortions make it less believable? Wasn't it more likely that the Gospel writers didn't really know what had happened? Why did God make his holy texts so hard to reconcile with one another, let alone other sources? How could Bill be so sure there was no problem when he wouldn't consider the details? Why did Gumbel not even attempt to address these contradictions in the course? How could anyone genuinely exploring the meaning of life take all this on trust?

We were not to know, because Bill suddenly drew things to a close. Afterwards he apologetically suggested a further debate in the pub some time, as if our line of questions wasn't suited to the discussion group. For now we wandered off, unenlightened – but with Jesus established as our only saviour, as far as the course was concerned.

Notes

1. *Questions of Life*, p.22. After delivering his preferred version of Josephus, Gumbel says, "So there is evidence outside the New Testament for the existence of Jesus."
2. That is, assuming one discounts the obviously forged section of Josephus that refers to the resurrection. Apologists like to point to Paul's epistles, in particular 1 Corinthians 15, as further evidence. However, these contain no biographical details of Jesus's life, only ideological assertions and vague second hand claims regarding the resurrection.
3. From the beginning of Christianity there were fundamental disputes

about what to believe. Indeed, these disputes heavily influenced which books were included in the Bible. An account of these disputes is given in Ehrman, B.D. (2005). *Lost Christianities: The Battles for Scripture and the Faiths We Never Knew*, OUP.

4. It is uncontroversial, even among Christians, that Matthew and Luke used Mark as a source. Some apologists recruit Paul, whose epistles were written before the Gospels, as an independent witness. However, there is no evidence that Paul met Jesus, and his epistles are starkly unilluminating about Jesus's life.

5. *Questions of Life*, p.21.

6. If Gumbel accepted 1 John 5:7-8 at face value he would surely include it in his discussion in *Searching Issues* of whether the Trinity is biblical. Instead he expends four pages (see chapter 7) quoting other Bible passages, never mentioning it. Since it is inconceivable that he doesn't know of the passage's existence his silence must indicate that he is aware of its dubious provenance.

7. See Ehrman, B.D. (2005). *Misquoting Jesus*, HarperCollins.

8. Mark 16:16, which says, "Whoever believes and is baptized will be saved, but whoever does not believe will be condemned", was probably not in the original manuscript, although that hasn't stopped Christians quoting it when convenient – see later. But this sentiment is hardly rare in the New Testament. In John 3:18 Jesus says, "Whoever believes in him [Jesus] is not condemned, but whoever does not believe stands condemned already because he has not believed in the name of God's one and only Son.". In Galatians 2:16 Paul makes clear that salvation can only come through "faith in Jesus Christ", not "by observing the law". Other relevant passages are Acts 16:30-31 and Romans 10:9. On page 26 of *Searching Issues* Gumbel is clear that Jesus is "the only way to God". On page 27 he stresses Jesus's unique status as the one who can save us, quoting Peter on the matter. Yet by pages 31-32 he is convinced that God's justness will win through, and that those who have never heard of Jesus can be saved. This is in plain contradiction to the passages cited above. Even if Gumbel could construct a basis for "great optimism", it would imply a self-contradictory or erroneous Bible.

9. *Questions of Life*, p.33.

10. *30 Days*, p.16.

11. Matthew 2:5-6.

12. Matthew 2:1 says "In the time of King Herod, after Jesus was born in Bethlehem of Judea, wise men from the East came to Jerusalem". Verse 2.3 has Herod alarmed at the birth.

13. Matthew 2:1 and Matthew 2:19-23.

14. Luke 2:1-4.

15. Matthew 2:16.

16. For a full discussion of the Gospel nativity accounts see Geza, V. (2006). *The Nativity*. Penguin.

17. See e.g. Luke 22:15.
18. NRSV translation. The NIV translation has "just before" but this choice was apparently motivated by a desire for Gospel consistency rather the original Greek. It does not in any case remove the problem of later verses still anticipating the Passover.
19. Geza, V. (2005) *The Passion*. Penguin. Vermes also supplies a list of other contradictions.
20. See, for instance, McDowell, J. & Stewart, D. (1999). *Answers to Tough Questions*. OM Publications.

CHAPTER 4

The Dojo Epiphany

We hadn't pinned down anything about Jesus, or about why he was worthy of faith. Alpha rests on the premise that he was the Son of God, yet only one week of the course is spent on this crucial question. We had skated over some unpersuasive evidence and left it there. But this wasn't going to derail the Alpha train: we were moving straight on to what the mysterious man had done for us. We were now to learn why Jesus died.

I thought I'd try to say less at the group this week; I wanted to hear more from the other group members, and my questions had obviously caused some irritation. Unfortunately it didn't really work out that way. If the welcome had seemed cool last week, the thermometer had definitely dropped further. Celia said hello and moved on quickly to her assigned "seeker". We were alone until we ran into Bill at the fruit juice stand. He seemed to struggle finding words for the ungodly, looking relieved when Pete, Anne and Sandy arrived. "I've been having a bad week," said Pete, looking down at his glass. He turned in my direction. "So," he said accusingly, "anything in your bag this week?"

Last time I'd brought a large annotated bible. I'd pulled it out when the question of who wrote the Gospel of Mark came up. Sandy had giggled, as if who wrote the words by which she lived her life was a question only for the nerdish obsessive. Analogies were apparently preferable for her and Pete. I decided not to tell them I'd brought Suetonius and Tacitus as well.

We drifted away and sat down on our own at one of the dinner tables, soon to be joined by a young Christian couple called Gordon and Elspeth. Thin and studious-looking, Gordon introduced himself confidently. He was a PhD student in particle physics, and seemed quite proud of it. His girlfriend, suffering from the usual Christian Union acne, was studying German and Spanish. They were doing non-student Alpha because they felt "much older" than their fellow students. They smiled at one another as they told us this.

Soon Gordon was describing his journey to faith. It had all started with ninjitsu, which he'd taken up after local hoodlums had put his friend in a headlock. During a spiritual test connected with his training he'd seen things that could only have supernatural explanations. He wouldn't reveal what these extraordinary happenings had been, but they'd spoken of a godly hand at work. He'd concluded that his atheistic father's "spouting" couldn't possibly be true.

The particular god he had found was supplied by Elspeth, a lifelong Christian. In the light of his dojo epiphany she had suggested he come along to church with her. Ever since then he had been a Christian. Wasn't it peculiar that these unearthly ninjitsu occurrences had pushed him toward Jesus instead of Eastern beliefs? Apparently not. It was, he said, as if he'd always believed crows were black until he'd seen a white one. This allusion to Karl Popper seemed strange, all things considered.[1]

Elspeth was more guarded, but we learned a little about her gap year in Germany. She'd spent it working in the kitchens at a company that translated missionary bibles. According to her, the previous session had been unnecessary: her culinary gap year had given her all the evidence she needed. The translators worked, she said, with all the original languages: "Hebrew, Greek and... err... Latin".[2]

Before we moved off to hear the talk, Gordon made a flower out of a napkin for Elspeth and left it on her plate while she was getting a cake. She seemed charmed, and made a little boat in return. Then Gordon made another flower, and said, "They're cheaper and last longer than real ones! Ha-ha!" We all chuckled together.

The lecture began with a humorous anecdote, this time from Tom. (He had done his research: not long ago the joke bagged second place in a scientific study to find the world's funniest joke.[3]) It was a version of the story that begins with two people camping in a tent with one asking the other "What do you see?" and ends "You idiot, someone's stolen our tent!" – except he'd made the characters Mike (the curate, giving the talk afterwards) and his wife. It went down even better than last week's joke, about a man accidentally taking up a challenge to swim the length of a shark-infested pool. As before, the warm up routine had no relation to the message of the evening, but the audience was loudly appreciative.

The evening's subject was sin. We are all invaded by the polluting, addictive horror that is sin, which "separates us from God". We all know what sin is, said Mike – murder, theft, child-molesting, etc. And we all need to do something about it because we are all, without exception, sinners. It isn't enough not to be armed robbers or murderers, because we are by definition sinful. By way of illustration he quoted Somerset Maugham: "If I wrote down every thought I have ever thought and every deed I have ever done, men would call me a monster of depravity". Immediately we'd jumped from obvious evils to far hazier crimes – some of them thought crimes, because it doesn't matter if we act on our ugly thoughts.[4] The trouble is, if ugly thoughts are in the same category as actual murder, what meaning does that category have? Do we, in fact, agree what sin is?

The great Christian thinkers are no obvious help. St Augustine, for instance, has a reputation for deep thought on the subject, yet his meditations are not entirely persuasive. Among other things, he considered that he had sinned as a newborn baby when he "cried too earnestly that I might suck [breastfeed]"[5] and by wanting to "play ball" more than do school work as a child.[6] This type of arbitrary pettiness is common in Evangelical Christian pronouncements on correct behaviour – unsurprisingly, since instilling a generalized feeling of guilt is an effective way of convincing people that they need Jesus's help. In his chapter on the subject, Gumbel is clear that he's taking on those who say because they lead "a good life" they "have no need of Christianity". They are wrong, of course, because they fall short of Jesus's perfection. They have engaged in "rebellion against God"; they have been "ignoring God in the sense of behaving as if he doesn't exist".[7] The resulting "pollution" can take many forms, including "evil thoughts, sexual immorality, theft, murder, adultery, greed, malice, deceit, lewdness, envy, slander, arrogance and folly".[8] More disturbing still, Gumbel emphasizes the view found in James 2:10 that "if we break *any* part of the Law we are guilty of breaking all of it".[9]

One might think, then, that we should pay very close attention to the Bible. It contains the Law, and we must follow every last rule; if we break a single one of them, it is as if we have broken them all. At times, Gumbel seems to agree. Later on he says "[t]he Bible should be our authority in all matters of 'creed and conduct'". On the Ten Commandments, he quotes a bishop saying that they "are a brilliant analysis of the minimum conditions on which a society, a people, a nation can live a sober, righteous and civilised life".[10] (That apparently means that stopping everyone working on the Sabbath is a minimum condition for living a "sober, righteous and civilised life".) But apart from these there are pages and pages of other, less known, laws, surely none of which can be ignored by the righteous. For example, Leviticus contains an array of sacred rulings on subjects ranging from eating weasels (11:29), to dealing with mildewed garments (13.47), to the ceremonial implications of "[w]hen a man has a discharge from his member" (15:2).[11] How could ignoring them fail to anger the Lord? It isn't as if Gumbel feels we can *generally* ignore the commandments in Leviticus – in *Searching Issues* he recruits that book's authority against occult practices.[12] The only attempt at an answer, not given in the course itself, is taken up in chapter 6.

Whatever sin is, the stakes could not be higher. Sin is not only bad, partitioning us from God; it is also addictive. Even basic emotions like anger are, Gumbel reveals, addictive, although how this relates to addiction as normally understood by psychologists is unclear. It is also hard to avoid recalling various Christians, avowedly propelled along by Christian love, who seem permanently angry. Ian Paisley, for instance, presumably should have booked into the Priory to sort out his anger addiction long ago. In any case, the overall message is clear: God has judged us for our sins, and the punishment is physical and spiritual death that "results in eternal isolation from God".[13] We can't work off the debt by trying to be good because the crime was too great.

It is very much a bad news/good news situation, though, because Jesus provides a get-out. He sacrificed himself to save us from our sins. Mike cited an earthly analogy: Father Maximilian Kolbe, a Polish Catholic priest, who in 1941 had bravely taken the place of a fellow Auschwitz prisoner, Franciszek Gajowniczek, who was to be executed. Kolbe had been killed by lethal injection after being left to starve for two weeks. Less admirable, and not mentioned by Gumbel, is the fact that Kolbe was a publisher of anti-Semitic articles before the war, in some small way encouraging the rise of the ideology that led to his murder. These anti-Semitic views led to protest when Pope John Paul II made him a saint in 1982.

Jesus, like Kolbe, had been through extreme suffering. He'd been whipped and flailed. He'd been spat upon. A battalion of six hundred soldiers had somehow all found the time to mock him.[14] Finally he'd stumbled under the weight of the cross to Golgotha where he'd been brutally nailed up and left to die. Mike stressed the cruelty of crucifixion, quoting Cicero on the subject. He pointed out, as Tom had the previous week, that the Romans often broke the condemned man's legs to speed his death (irrelevantly, because we know from John that this didn't happen to Jesus[15]).

Whatever his history, Father Kolbe's sacrifice was impressive. He'd exchanged his life for someone else's. The case of Jesus is less clear. Firstly, the sacrifice was decidedly temporary: however painful his death, he was resurrected after three days. Secondly, the sacrifice was of God to God: it was, in the Alpha Course manual's words, a "self-sacrifice". The idea that God "gave his only son" was false in any normal sense, a play on words evoking human feelings not applicable to a father whose son was a personification of himself. Thirdly, why had we sinned in the first place? Wasn't it ultimately God's fault if he created us along with our inevitable sin? If he'd arranged a situation where he knew sin was bound to occur, and he judged us for that sin, it didn't seem unreasonable for him to deal with the problem. I didn't see a magnified form of Kolbe's sacrifice, as Mike claimed. I saw a God who had played a bizarre game with himself, beyond our control, and apparently expected us to be deeply thankful for the result.

God created sin, judged the sin that he'd created to be bad, sacrificed himself to himself for the sin that he'd created but nonetheless judged to be bad – and we were to be grateful because the responsibility for the sin that God had created rested on us because we'd done the sinning (except that humans are by their God-given nature incapable of not sinning). Now we had to try, and inevitably fail, to adhere to his rules in order to show our gratitude for this, but it didn't matter how badly we failed provided we repented because Jesus had taken away our sins. The idea of the Trinity appears as a monumental linguistic fudge designed to cover up a nonsensical position.

The analogy given by Mike of a judge who, instead of recusing himself, sentenced his friend to a fine ("justice") and then wrote him a cheque for that fine ("love"), was not altogether persuasive. What justice was there when the criminal paid no price himself? Was it right for a judge to rule on crimes that he himself had set in train? Was God really so loving to selectively commute the universal death sentence he had imposed? It wasn't as if we had ever had a chance to escape it by our own efforts. It wasn't even as if original sin stemmed from any crime of our own.

If Mike had a logical explanation it was invisible amid the murk of parables and, finally, pure emotion. At the end of the talk he intoned repeatedly that Jesus had "died for you… he died for YOU… he died for me… he died for you". The sermon became a chant, intensely affecting the people around me. They stared fixedly at Mike as I wondered if it would all end with the downward arc of a sacrificial dagger.

Suddenly it all came to a halt, and we were instructed to join our groups. Mike encouraged everybody to ask questions, but looking at the wide-eyed audience they seemed unlikely to be penetrating ones.

By the time I'd joined the group the introductions were almost finished. The make-up of the group had changed this week. Vague Wilma and Dr Phillip were missing, but there were several new additions. Next to me was Belinda, a plump middle-aged Irish woman whose faith didn't seem altogether solid, and an Armenian woman named Nadine with big hair – another waverer. A new band of committed Christians had also been drafted in. There was a couple who'd just come back from Italy (they'd been to the Vatican) – he was a tree surgeon, she a musician – and an aggressive looking young balding man named Martin whose earring and not-quite-trendy clothes somehow suggested he liked Christian dance music.

"So, what were everyone's impressions of the talk?" asked a smiling Bill. He nodded earnestly as the various Christians described the power of Jesus's sacrifice. It was, said the musician, "mind-blowing… when you think of what he did for us". Previously she'd had more of an image of God as judge, but the talk had revealed his sensitive side. Her boyfriend was jealous because he wasn't coming fresh to the extraordinary sacrifice. He'd got blasé about it, so he envied recently born again Christians. Hearing Father Kolbe's story had brought the awesome reality back into focus. Pete agreed: during the Father Kolbe tale the "hairs stood up" on his arm. His cynicism had left him.

The conversation went on like this for about ten minutes. It felt as if saying anything not sufficiently awestruck would ruin the atmosphere. Everything was founded on the Gospel Passion narrative, but we hadn't established even that was accurate, let alone all the sacrificial theology. Instead we had fervent emotion – the musician sometimes seemed on the edge of tears.

Eventually Malc broke the spell by asking whether Jesus dying two thousand years ago had a bearing on sins today. Pete muttered sarcastically, "Oh, I'd almost given up on you". He seemed convinced we were conspiring to ruin the group. Bill seemed equally unimpressed. "Jesus's sacrifice was eternal," he answered abruptly.

The question of the definition of sin then came up. "Was it", I wondered, "what the Bible told us not to do?"

"What do you mean?" asked Bill.

I couldn't see how to make the general question any clearer so I raised a specific point. There were rules in the Bible that people appeared to be ignoring right now – women being prohibited from speaking in church for example.[16] Could these rules be ignored?

"You know there's some context around that passage, don't you?" asked Bill.

He didn't volunteer the context, so I raised another example: "There are a lot of things banned in the Bible that people today don't necessarily think are wrong. So I wonder about those. To take another example, Paul says women should cover their hair in church."[17] (Later in the same passage Paul also says that "…if a man has long hair, it is a disgrace to him". If this was so then Malc, with his shoulder length hair, should immediately be asked to leave the church until he had a less ungodly haircut.)

"What do YOU think about that?" said the Leader, in an unfriendly fashion.

"Well as I say, I'm not sure what a sin is if we can ignore some things in the Bible. We all agree murder is wrong, but what about some of these other things? Is the Bible our guide here?"

Bill didn't seem keen on giving his own views as we went round this cycle several times. He seemed to have adopted a Jesus-style tactic of throwing everything back as a question. Sandy eventually intruded a suggestion: "If you're fascinated by women covering their hair there was a sermon on it – perhaps we can dig it out."

"I'm not particularly interested in it. It's just an example. I'm trying to work out which parts of the Bible we can ignore."

"We can't ignore them," was the immediate reply. Except that it was from a woman, who was prohibited to speak as far as I could see. Nadine then equally sinfully said that women in the Armenian Church did cover their hair. The idea that this issue was just one example was lost. In *Searching Issues* Gumbel says, "As we read Scripture, we need to open our hearts and minds to things we may not want to hear, and perhaps to wrestle with the gap between the experience of our own desires and the reality of biblical teaching."[18] He says this in his section on homosexuality, where he quotes 1 Corinthians 6:9-10 against the practice. Yet as far as I could tell, Gumbel and everyone in our group were failing to open their hearts and minds, failing to wrestle with Paul's clear words elsewhere in 1 Corinthians. How could they, without providing any explanation, so easily discard these rules?

"Again, it's just an example, but a more important example is homosexuality. Is that wrong?" I asked.[19]

"What do you think is wrong?" asked Bill. If he'd read *Searching Issues* then he knew the Alpha view was that homosexuality was indeed a sin, but he refused to say either way.[20] Martin agreed with Gumbel, although he didn't see fit to debate this with the other Christians there – a united front was being presented. "All sins are equal," he told me.

"So homosexuality is as bad as… murder?" I asked. He confirmed that it was, but the other Christians were careful to keep their silence – Martin had seemingly strayed off message. (On a side note, denial of the Holy Spirit is described in the Bible as the only unforgivable sin.[21] This suggests that all sins are in fact not equal.) Rather than discuss Martin's extreme pronouncement, we segued without any explicit disagreement to Anne's more touchy-feely conception of sin. Her view was that you had to consult your heart.

"So if we feel it's OK in our heart can we go against rules in the Bible?" I asked, hoping we'd established a rule.

"A sin," Anne announced, "is what takes you further from God." There were nods from Pete and others. I let the matter drop – the group seemed to be getting increasingly hostile.

For a while I sat pondering what it all meant. Bill had discarded any pretence of friendliness, entirely, as far as I could see, because my questions betrayed an unacceptable level of scepticism. I didn't think I'd been particularly combative. While questions were allowed, it seemed they were only welcome if they propelled us to the correct conclusion. In fact, Gumbel's book on running the course espouses exactly this view: "Even if someone says something that is not correct, a good leader will respond with a phrase like, 'How interesting', or 'I have never heard that before, or 'It might mean that…', and will then bring in the rest of the group to try to reach the right conclusion."[22] The "right conclusion" was, ultimately, the one that brought people to Alpha Christianity – evidence and logic were not the operative factors. But it could never be revealed how or why we were "incorrect": that would detract from the friendly, open, exploratory feel to the discussion.

Soon enough Malc raised another issue. What was the relation of the Old Testament to the New Testament, given their sharply differing views on acceptable behaviour? Bill and friends again acted as if it was a strange question. "I think we just need to follow the Ten Commandments," Anne suggested.

Nadine confessed she always muddled the Ten Commandments with the Seven Deadly Sins. Anne said she'd studied them at school, and in fact the Seven Deadly Sins came from a nineteenth century play.[23]

"Following the Ten Commandments seems reasonable enough, as far as it goes, but what about all the other rules in the Old Testament?" I foolishly asked Bill.

"What other rules?" he retorted, as if his masters degree in theology and years as a Christian had left him ignorant of the large body of Mosaic Law.

"Leviticus has all these rules – some of them are hard to follow today. Can we ignore those?"

"Which rules?"

"Well, for instance there are two chapters on what to do about skin complaints…"[24]

"What did Jesus tell us about the Ten Commandments?" Bill retorted, eyes gleaming.

"He told us to love our neighbour and he told us to love no other God."

"Right!" said The Leader, clearly feeling a victory had been won.

"But does that cover everything? What about the other stuff? Can it be ignored?" I naively persisted.

"What other stuff?"

"Well as I say, these skin complaint rules, or many other things…" I began.

"Which other things?"

"Well OK, like the rule that people must check their chair hasn't been sat on by a menstruating woman".[25] Sandy began making disgusted faces at Anne. "Or the idea that if people have been made unclean by various means they can't approach the altar. This is in Leviticus, right?" He admitted it was, but didn't seem interested in suggesting an answer.

Sandy could no longer contain herself: "What is YOUR view? You ask so many questions – YOU must have a view." Her enraged tone gave the strong impression that these were not good things.

I said that I couldn't see how to reconcile the brutal, ritual-obsessed God of the Old Testament, who killed so many people, with the loving personal God in the New Testament.

"What do you mean specifically?" asked Bill.

"Well there are pages and pages of smiting," I insisted. Bill didn't agree or disagree. "The Old Testament God seems genocidal… sexist… I can't make it fit with the New Testament."

Nadine was surprised: "He killed all these people?"

"Some he killed directly, some deaths he just ordered." It has been estimated that God is responsible for upwards of 2.25 million recorded deaths in the Bible.[26] Satan, fount of all evil, is reported to have killed ten.

All this time Sandy had been madly pointing at her watch, apparently uninterested in the reply to her question, so Bill shut the discussion down.

Again we seemed to have learned little from Alpha this week: the session had simply raised more questions. We had not been able to decide on what was and was not a sin, and without this the need for

Jesus's baffling sacrifice was unclear. On the one hand it seemed it should just be a matter of consulting the Bible, and the Christians in our group agreed that no rule in the Bible should be ignored. On the other hand, they were ignoring inconvenient rules, or worse were ignorant of what the Bible actually said. Even granted a clear definition of sin, we hadn't even had time to address the meaning of the crucifixion. Why did Jesus die? It was impossible to say.

Notes

1. The standard example of Karl Popper's idea of falsification is the theory that all swans are white. Sight of a black swan would immediately disprove, or *falsify*, that theory. Was Gordon saying evidence-based reasoning was itself falsifiable? Apart from the philosophical implications, where did it leave Gordon's study of physics? The full implications of a gladly adopted premise were, as so often in Alpha, simply left to one side.
2. There is no Latin in the Bible.
3. The British Association for the Advancement of Science. (2002). *Laughlab: the scientific quest for the world's funniest joke.* Arrow Books, London.
4. Jesus pronounced in Matthew 5:28 that anyone with lustful thoughts had already committed adultery.
5. Sir Tobie Mathew (translator). *The Confessions of St Augustine.* (1923). Fontana Books, London, p.38 (Book 1, Chapter 7).
6. Ibid., p.43, (Book 1, Chapter 10).
7. *Questions of Life*, p.40.
8. Ibid., p.41. Gumbel is quoting Jesus speaking in Mark 7:20-23.
9. Ibid., p.41. Note that the "Law" referred to here is specifically that of the Old Testament.
10. Ibid., p.74.
11. NRSV translation.
12. *Searching Issues*, p.56.
13. *Questions of Life*, p.42. Here Gumbel and Mark quoted Romans 6:23: "For the wages of sin is death, but the free gift of God is eternal life in Christ Jesus our Lord."
14. The figure of 600 isn't explicitly given by the Gospels. Matthew and Mark report a company or cohort of soldiers, which is estimated to be up to 600 men.
15. See John 19:32-33.
16. Corinthians 14: 34-35 states that "women should remain silent in the churches. They are not allowed to speak, but must be in submission, as the Law says. If they want to inquire about something, they should ask their own husbands at home; for it is disgraceful for a woman to speak in the church."

17. In 1 Corinthians 11:3-5 Paul expounds at length on this issue: "...the head of every man is Christ, and the head of the woman is man...every woman who prays or prophesies with her head uncovered dishonours her head" – and so on until verse 16.
18. *Searching Issues*, p.72.
19. In Leviticus 18:22 we are told, "Do not lie with a man as one lies with a woman; that is detestable". If you do "the land... will vomit you out" for defiling it (18:28). In Romans 1:26-27 Paul reaffirms this sentiment, generalising the horror to lesbian activity.
20. In *Searching Issues*, page 72, Gumbel states "God's context for sexual intercourse is lifelong commitment (in marriage) between one man and one woman (Genesis 2:24). This view of marriage and sex, which Jesus quoted and endorsed, rules out all sex outside marriage, whether heterosexual or homosexual." He is certain that "biblical writers clearly disapprove of same-sex sexual practices." All this is after vowing on page 71 to "resist all forms of irrational prejudice."
21. Matthew 12:31-32: "And so I tell you, every sin and blasphemy will be forgiven men, but the blasphemy against the Spirit will not be forgiven. Anyone who speaks a word against the Son of Man will be forgiven, but anyone who speaks against the Holy Spirit will not be forgiven, either in this age or in the age to come." Mark 3:29: "But whoever blasphemes against the Holy Spirit can never have forgiveness, but is guilty of an eternal sin".
22. *How to Run the Alpha Course*, p.139.
23. I later learned that the idea had existed for many centuries.
24. See Leviticus 13 and 14 for a lengthy description.
25. The Old Testament is stringent and detailed on the subject of menstruation. Leviticus 15:19-20: "When a woman has her regular flow of blood, the impurity of her monthly period will last seven days, and anyone who touches her will be unclean till evening. Anything she lies on during her period will be unclean, and anything she sits on will be unclean." Leviticus 20:18: "If a man lies with a woman during her monthly period and has sexual relations with her, he has exposed the source of her flow, and she has also uncovered it. Both of them must be cut off from their people." Ezekiel 18:5-9: "Suppose there is a righteous man who does what is just and right - He does not... lie with a woman during her period... – That man is righteous; he will surely live, declares the sovereign LORD."
26. This figure only includes those Biblical stories that report numbers of deaths. There are also almost 40 additional massacres in which an unreported number of people are killed, such as the destruction of Sodom and Gomorrah, and the famous flood that killed everyone on earth except Noah and his wife. See Appendix B for more detailed information.

CHAPTER 5

The Real Mount Sinai is a Military Base

Bill and other Christians had implied that certainty would never be found in the search for Christianity – a "leap of faith" wasn't a certain thing. This week's talk was nevertheless called "How can I be sure of my faith?", but it consisted of indicators of belief, not foundations for it – reassurance rather than proof. There was little for the sceptic who began with no faith.

Was Alpha really trying to persuade anyone, or just affirm prejudices? Sandy had seemed offended by the idea of serious debate. I decided to ask Anne, who was in high spirits because it was her reading week. Was I right in thinking there had been a bad atmosphere last week? Were my questions at fault? She wavered, keen to reassure me that everything was OK, but also admitting the group wasn't going as well as she'd like. Eventually she decided everything was fine, and that I shouldn't worry. What about Sandy's attitude at the last meeting – the way my questions had seemed to send her into a boiling fury? This was just the way of Sandy, apparently: "You have to get to know her." Further discussion along previous lines seemed unlikely to facilitate this.

After we sat down, Anne revealed some of her own worries. She had to walk a line of convincingly answering people's questions and suggesting instructive examples, but without making it obvious she was a helper. A shill's life was difficult. She confirmed that every group had a bogus waverer like her, and from talking to the others she'd learned things were going more smoothly elsewhere. What was wrong with our group?

She was also disappointed with the large fall in numbers since the Alpha Supper. From counting the tables it seemed over half the original attendees had gone, and much of the remainder had already been saved when they'd arrived. She mused about the retention troubles: "What we've found is unless they really click with someone on the first day they don't come back. It depends so much on who we place with people." Part of the Alpha strategy was centrally planned dinner companionship.

I wanted to know more, but she'd already defended the shill concept and it was difficult to probe further. She was there, she said, so that there was someone around who was more approachable than the Leader. The unspoken element was that this approachable person also had to have the right opinions. It still seemed like something you'd expect at a timeshare presentation, not an honest inquiry into the meaning of life. Anne occasionally seemed embarrassed as she said all this, but clearly felt it was all worthwhile if it brought the unbeliever to God.

When conversation lulled she beckoned the Leader over and immediately things became more awkward. He seemed deeply suspicious, and the only subject that piqued his interest was Malc's recent holiday in Egypt. He jumped on my suggestion that Malc was visiting Mount Sinai. Bill was clear: Mount Sinai isn't in Egypt; the one there is a fake for tourists.

The evidence for claiming any mountain as the biblical Mount Sinai is inevitably flimsy because the surrounding geography has to be inferred from oblique scriptural mentions. Like most alleged physical evidence for biblical truth there are huge gaps, even assuming the Old Testament was accurate in what it recorded. Who is to say anything from the Exodus story bears any relation to reality? Stories in this part of the Bible were apparently inspired by prevalent myths at the time (e.g. the flood). The uneven language and content indicates they were spliced together (there are two creation stories for this reason, written by people with different words for "God"), and then edited over centuries by multiple scribes. Nobody can say if Moses existed, let alone received the Commandments on a mountain, let alone which mountain it might have been.

Bill was untroubled by these concerns. "The real Mount Sinai is a military base," he told me. "It's in Saudi Arabia. The trouble is they have it all fenced off." He leaned forward with a sly look on his face. "And you have to wonder why."

What was he was implying? Did he think the Saudis were covering up the truth about Moses to spite the Christian faith? Weren't they interested in the tourist dollars Egypt was getting? Didn't Muslims also revere Moses? Bill wouldn't be drawn – he seemed to think he'd already said too much.

Eventually we got on to the problems with the group. Bill was less encouraging than Anne. He reiterated his sympathy for my position, on account of once being a sceptic himself, but didn't deny that there had been bad feeling in the group session. He again stressed openness to questions, but he didn't seem to want them in the group, because he again suggested the pub as the place to discuss them. Fundamental objections to the Christian faith just weren't, it seemed, what Alpha groups were all about.

Bill then told me about his "personal journey". He emphasized his questioning background. He had been a military planner in the air force, and was now an analyst at his company. He was logical, and he'd been unable to come to Christianity through his mind. Fortunately he'd made a "leap of faith", and immediately afterwards he had, he said joyfully, been "showered in grace". But that didn't mean Christianity wasn't rational – he insisted it was.

It seemed a persistent theme, the combination of what were always termed "academic" or "intellectual" aspects with "spiritual" or "emotional" ones. In spite of the earlier claims to be "drowning" in evidence, and the idea that Jesus is outstandingly well-attested historically, the implication seemed to be that evaluating the evidence rationally would never be enough to bring people Jesus: they had to make an irrational leap too. Except nobody would own up to it being irrational – there was always some other hazy category, not rational and not irrational.

The sermon this week was less electrifying than the last one – even the anecdote was boring. In revenge for the tent-stealing hilarity of the previous week, Mike bore false witness that Tom had been duped by an old lady in Tesco, and she'd taken advantage of his good nature to get him to pay for her shopping. The audience tittered.

There were three basic strands to Tom's message of reassurance. First there was God's promise of eternal life. Second, we could look to Jesus's death on the cross for our sins (covered last week). And third, there was the "witness" of the Holy Spirit. The "God's promise" section quoted a selection of reassuring statements from the deity. We didn't learn about his wrathful side – for instance when he tried (and, bewilderingly, failed) to kill Moses, apparently for having an uncircumcised son by a foreign woman (Exodus 4:24-26).[1] Instead we had the heart-warming fatherly bits: he is knocking at the (spiritual) door, waiting for us to let him in (Revelation 3:20); he is with us always (Matthew 28:20); he came to give abundant life (John 10:10); and so on. It was partly a re-run of the previous week, and the sacrifice of Jesus still made little sense even with the comforting New Testament quotations on the subject. There was no new evidence to encourage us to believe in the resurrection accounts.

One new aspect was the recruitment of Jesus as a shield against charges of arrogance. The triumphant Christian book title *Heaven, Here I come* was not arrogant, we were told, because Christians were not destined for Heaven on their own account; it was all Jesus's doing. This didn't quite put them in the clear, in my view, as any certainty of being heaven-bound surely still reflected a certain belief that they had pleased God enough to secure entry,[2] leaving aside apparently equally certain views of the Bible's truth and meaning.

"What is faith?" asks Nicky Gumbel in *Questions of Life*, before supplying a couple of gladdening anecdotes by way of illustration.[3] One is about John Gibson Paton, a nineteenth century Scottish missionary to Vanuatu (then called the New Hebrides). Seeking to translate the New Testament, he cast around for a suitable term to convey belief or trust in God:

"One day when his native servant came in, Paton raised both feet off the floor, sat back in his chair and asked, 'What am I doing now?' In reply, the servant used a word which means, 'to lean your whole weight upon'. This was the expression Paton used. Faith is leaning our whole weight upon Jesus and what he has done for us on the cross."

Paton was a man of strong faith. Another admiring Christian source[4] describes his battle to persuade the British Admiralty that this was all he needed to face down savage cannibals:

'Finally one of the sea lords urged that Paton be allowed to go. "If they eat him," he said, "it will give us an excuse to blow the islands out of the sea." Paton retorted that he had some gunpowder of his own he wanted to try first. He was referring to the Word of God. Later, when a British Royal Commission visited the islands after Paton had evangelized them, it reported that the natives of the New Hebrides were amongst the happiest and most enlightened peoples under the British flag.'

Paton did try his Word of God gunpowder, but it failed, so he used real gunpowder instead. In 1865, finding his message falling on stony ground, he called in HMS Curaçoa to deliver the Good News more forcefully. Despite the Tannese having committed no specific crime, at Paton's request the Curaçoa bombarded 15 villages around the mission station and landed marines and sailors on the island to set the villages on fire and destroy every canoe they could find. One of the ship's lieutenants condemned Paton for the "unctuous language of cant", and he was criticized by other missionaries at the time,[5] but it is difficult to find any mention of this incident in Christian literature today.[6] Instead this man, who clearly leaned at least some of his weight on naval artillery rather than Jesus, is held up as a model of bravery and faith. Christian outlets still carry inspiring biographies with titles like "John G. Paton: Hero of the South Seas". HMS Curaçoa isn't mentioned.[7]

Paton is supposed to exemplify "The Work of Jesus", but perhaps he should have relied on the "Witness of the Spirit" – another reason for faith. The Spirit is intimately involved with every Alpha Christian's life. It makes them "more loving, more joyful, more peaceful, more patient, more kind, and more self-controlled".[8] It also apparently makes some of them turn up the radio when they hear the word "Jesus".[9] The amazing change in converts from unpleasant pessimism and cynicism to Christian cheeriness seemed to be the closest the talk came to supplying any observable evidence for Christianity's truth.

The jollity of, say Deepak Chopra's adherents, suggests that Christianity isn't the only route to faith-based happiness or contentment. The truth of a belief doesn't have much to do with the happiness it might bring. As George Bernard Shaw famously said, "The fact that a believer is happier than a skeptic is no more to the point than the fact that a drunken man is happier than a sober one". But in any case I wasn't convinced that belief in Christianity could ultimately bring much happiness. It would mean believing in a god who had slaughtered innocents in their millions, sent down horrific diseases, and repeatedly failed to intervene in natural disasters and wars. Not only would one have to accept this being's existence, but one would have to believe he was in fact very loving, in spite of his obvious lack of interest in earthly suffering, and his forthright consignment of the majority of humanity to a lake of fiery sulphur (Revelation 21:8).[10]

Even pushing aside these problems, as most Christians seem to, a new class of potential troubles awaits. As far as consolation goes, trust in God is not single-edged. There are entire books designed to address specifically Christian psychological problems.[11] Commonly these revolve around sin, a sense of which Mike had worked hard to instil earlier. Trust in God can lead to depression, because his well-documented failures to intervene can easily lead to feelings of guilt on the part of those expecting help. If somebody is a fervent Christian, and God fails to step in despite their hope and expectation, who can they blame but themselves? It must be down to their sin. Such outcomes of Christian faith are not part of the Alpha syllabus.

The overarching theme was that Christians just lead nicer lives, which somehow means that they can be "sure" of their beliefs. But if, in spite of all this, some members of the congregation still doubted, all they needed was to say a prayer. "If you are unsure about whether you have ever really believed in Jesus," Gumbel and Tom concluded, "here is a prayer which you can pray as a way of starting the Christian life and receiving all the benefits which Jesus died to make possible." The congregation intoned in unison a standard bid for forgiveness, and a request for the Heavenly Father to "be with me for ever". God would then enter their hearts and short-circuit any inconvenient thinking.

Prayer took up a lot of the group's time. Bill asked what we thought prayer was, and Martin, the angry bearded Christian, had a smirking reply ready: it was "like having a chinwag with God".

The vague woman, Wilma, thought it was a bit selfish to pray for oneself all the time. And she wasn't convinced that God was very interested in helping his followers pick the best house to buy. These seemed legitimate concerns, but Christians weren't worried: there were sympathetic nods but also polite disagreements. They seemed to feel their house hunting had indeed benefited from divine guidance.

"How do you feel about God?" Bill asked Wilma, as usual asking for an open-ended restatement when an opinion he didn't like was expressed.

"I think there's something there… but I'm not sure about him helping with buying houses. He must have better things to do…"

Bill appeared doubtful. Wilma seemed embarrassed.

The committed Christian faction didn't agree about the selfishness. Anne's comment settled it: "His shoulders are broad enough."

Sandy seemed surprised by my silence through all this. "Surely YOU have a question about this? YOU'VE been very silent. What do YOU think about prayer?" she demanded.

I hesitated. "I was wondering, with all this talk of prayer, how God responds to it? I mean, how does he answer it?"

"What do you mean?" asked Bill in his habitual way.

"Well I don't know what the normal view is. Does he intervene directly, or work through people? How do you know if your prayer's been answered?"

There was silence for a while. "I don't think there is a normal view," Bill eventually said. It seemed quite an important aspect of prayer to me, but not to him. He wanted to move on to forgiveness. While we had to pray for those who sinned against us, we didn't have to trust them. He'd found this very comforting, he said, although I wasn't sure what it meant. Then Bill raised a controversial question: "Would Hitler have gone to heaven if he'd repented?"

Anne pointed out that God saw all sinners as the same. Bill nodded. Had they scripted this exchange? His view was that God's grace was infinite, so anybody could be forgiven. He couldn't be sure about Hitler, though, as it was "between him and God".

Again the Christian judicial system seemed decidedly strange. It didn't matter if you were a mass murderer or a one-time adulterer in thought only: you were all the same to God. It was hard to understand why he had these personal "chinwags" with people if he took such a minimal interest in what they'd done. Was he spending too much time on house hunting?

Pete told us about his Christian awakening since he'd started the Alpha Course. All it had taken was a brief read of C.S.Lewis's *Mere Christianity* ("Great book by the way!") to convince him. Suddenly he put a compelling argument to me: "Going back to what you were saying two weeks ago. He says that 99% of what we believe in life we have to take on trust. Like we get on an aeroplane and we don't know if it'll work. We don't know what an electron is. We just have to trust."

"My answer to that… the question I'd ask in reply is what authority do we trust when there's more than one and they disagree? I mean, we have Christian authorities telling us one thing, and Muslim authorities telling us another…" (Perhaps a more important objection is that there is fundamental difference between empirical scientific laws and religious belief.)

Martin wasn't having this: "I believe in my God and when I die I'll find out."

"But if we get it wrong, we could burn in a lake of sulphur…"

"If I'm wrong then I won't go to heaven."

"So it pays to get it right, yeah?"

He didn't reply, so Sandy contributed her own theory: "It's like one of those children's games with different shaped holes and pegs. You just have to find which one fits."

This didn't seem to settle the problem, because it didn't say why the one that fitted was the right one. We'd just spoken about the consequences if it was wrong. What did this "fitting" mean, when billions of humans "fitted" other, contradictory belief systems? Besides, as Wilma pointed out, "Surely your religion comes from where you're born?"

Bill didn't think so. "I agree that used to be the case, but not so much today. There was a man in Somalia, which is mainly Muslim… he walked four hundred miles to Addis Ababa to get a Bible. Imagine that – four hundred miles! So I don't think that's true anymore."

It didn't seem conclusive proof. The statistical correlation between country of upbringing and religion strongly points in the other direction – but raising that point, I thought, would perhaps have been nitpicking, and that was not allowed in Alpha.

In any case, Bill then drew the session to a close. On my way out Pete said, "Thanks Stuart. See you next week." I was surprised he'd thanked me, but there again, nothing I said seemed likely to change his mind, so why not? He was sure of his faith.

Notes

1. The mother averted God's wrath via emergency surgery. See Appendix B for more examples.
2. Under the doctrine of predestination adopted by some Protestant factions this particular criticism would not hold, but it would instead be necessary to believe that one's salvation had been divinely ordained before birth. The arrogance remains.
3. *Questions of Life*, p.59. Note: Gumbel spells Paton's name as "Patton".
4. Phillips, J. (2002). *100 Old Testament Sermon Outlines*. Kregel, p.83. The anecdote is billed as an illustration of "The Invincible Word of God".
5. Others approved his methods. The Curaçoa next stopped at the nearby island of Erromango, which was bombarded at the request of another missionary, a Reverend Gordon, who despite the destruction of the village of Sifu did not feel the navy had done enough. There was also the disastrous intervention of HMS Favourite, under the command of William Croker, at Tonga in 1840 at the request of the missionaries there. Civil war had broken out when most of the Tongan population opposed the missionary backed Christianised Tongan leader, "King George". Believing the Christian cause was "more important than his professional career" Croker was killed immediately in a farcical "heroic" charge against a Tongan fort which also resulted in the capture of the ships guns on the beach. The missionaries quickly disowned him.
6. For descriptions of all these events see: Tucker, R. (2004). *From Jerusalem to Irian Jaya: A Biographical History of Christian Missions*. p.226; Samson, J. (1998) *Imperial Benevolence: Making British Authority in the Pacific Islands*. University of Hawaii Press, Honolulu; Lightner, S. & Naupa, A. (2005) *Histri Blong Yumi Long Vanuatu: Volume 2*. Vanuatu National Cultural Council, Port Vila.
7. Neither was the hypocrisy of the attacks lost on the islanders, who initially rejected the reestablishment of the mission after the bombardment, complaining that the missionaries had "told them it was wrong to fight, and advised them to give up their wars, and then brought a man-of-war to kill them and destroy their property" (cited in Samson 1998).
8. *Questions of Life*, p.62.
9. Ibid., p.63.
10. Revelation 21:8: "But the cowardly, the unbelieving, the vile, the murderers, the sexually immoral, those who practise magic arts, the idolaters and all liars – their place will be in the fiery lake of burning sulphur. This is the second death."
11. See, for example, Nelson, M. (1974). *Why Christians Crack Up*, Hodder and Stoughton.

CHAPTER 6

Stuff about Periods

I arrived at session four of the Alpha course on my own, as Malc had found a more pressing matter to attend to than saving his soul. Martin, the angry bearded soundman, greeted me with a sarcastic-sounding "hi" and immediately walked off. He was soon replaced by the tree surgeon and music teacher who had found Jesus's sacrifice on the cross mind-blowing a couple of weeks previously. The music teacher quizzed me suspiciously about my church background.

As ever, the talk began with an anecdote the punch-line of which was obvious from the first sentence, this time delivered by Tom. Mike had tried to sell his car, which had a lot of miles on the clock. His clever but criminal wife had suggested clocking it, which he did, whereupon dim old Mike had decided to keep it because – guess what! – he thought it was a good car now it had a low mileage. All through, the audience guffawed, seemingly more at the thought that their dear curate could be so very naughty than the joke itself. When Mike got up to deliver the sermon he retaliated with another over-before-it-started joke (a woman reading "A Tale of Two Cities" had twins, another reading "The Three Musketeers" had triplets...). Then we were on to a serious matter: How and why should we read the Bible?

We should read it because of the three Ps.[1] Mike emphasized the amazing *popularity* of the Good Book. Not only is it a bestseller – 44 million copies sold a year – but the average American household inexplicably has 6.8 bibles. Of course, popularity isn't a wholly reliably measure of godliness, or Nicky Gumbel wouldn't have written a book attacking *The Da Vinci Code*. Luckily, the Bible is also uniquely *powerful* and *precious*: powerful because it allows us access to God, and precious because Gumbel once gave away a copy to a citizen of the USSR who ran "down the street jumping for joy".

Given the Bible's precious powerful popularity, we need to know how to apply it to our daily lives, and here Alpha is categorical: it is a "manual for life".[23] Gumbel is clear that the Bible is *the* guide on how to live one's life. He calls it "God's rule book",[4] "the supreme authority for what we believe and how we act",[5] where we are told "what we can do and what we must not do".[6] It is in the Bible, Gumbel says, "that we find out what is wrong in God's eyes and how we can live a righteous life". Mike directed us to a passage from 2 Timothy,[7] whose author is clear that scripture is divinely inspired – literally, "theopneustos" or "God-breathed". So although humans wrote the Bible, the content is very much God's.[8] It is therefore our authority for "teaching, rebuking, correcting and training in righteousness".[9] I had failed in my attempt to train the women of our group in the righteousness of silence in church. This warranted further discussion in the group – possibly even a rebuke.

Because the Bible was divinely inspired it follows that scripture is inerrant. At least, this is what Gumbel strongly implies but shies from explicitly stating.[10] He says that this has been the "universal view of the worldwide church" throughout history, as well as that of Church Father Ireneaus, Luther and Catholic doctrine. He also admits that there are "difficult" passages, and suggests that they can be explained by "historical context", but what this means – whether this means the Bible is not in fact infallible, whether we can in fact ignore certain biblical rules – is never spelled out.[11] The subject is not covered in *Questions of Life*, and nobody we spoke to was interested in discussing it – an amazing fact, given the volume of bizarre biblical edicts and the strong claims made in the course. The only Alpha answer, confined to the Old Testament part of the question, is crammed into an endnote of *Challenging Lifestyle*, a follow-up book:

"The Old Testament law can be divided more or less into three categories. First, there is the moral law. These injunctions are broad and generally applicable to all societies (e.g. the Ten Commandments). This law still applies to us today. Secondly, the Old Testament also includes what might loosely be described as the "civil law": laws which are more specific and directed to the particular social problems of ancient Israel. Although the principles underlying these laws are valid and authoritative for the Christian, the particular applications found in the Old Testament may not be… As well as moral and civil law there is also ceremonial law in the Old Testament. The writer of Hebrews deals very thoroughly with the uncleanliness regulations and the sacrificial rituals of the Old Testament. The effect of his argument is that the practice of the ceremonial law is obsolete for the Christian."[12]

Things are not as simple as Gumbel asserts. For a start, this neat classification system was by no means settled in the first centuries of Christianity, when the idea of discarding Jewish Law was deeply controversial. One sect, the Marcionites, discarded the entire Old Testament. Another, the Ebionites, enforced almost all its rules, and insisted on circumcision.[13] Naturally these people were denounced as heretics by people with views between these extremes, some of whom eventually succeeded in imposing the ruling orthodoxy. But the fundamental disagreement they exemplify is hardly surprising, because nowhere in the Bible is any such classification scheme announced or directly implied, even though the Bible canon was chosen by the winners of the dispute. (The current view of which texts were divinely inspired was not shared by Marcionites or Ebionites, who had radically different positions. Disagreement about which books belong in the Bible continues today – see below.)

In fact the New Testament contains evidence of a dispute between followers of Jesus who imposed Jewish rites and those who wanted to relax those restrictions. In Galatians 2:11 Paul says he opposed Peter's imposition of Jewish customs on followers. Acts 15 describes key disciples debating the issue. Christians typically point to this chapter to justify abandoning Jewish Law, because in it Peter apparently comes round to Paul's view, refers to Jewish Law as "a yoke that neither we nor our fathers have been able to bear", and suggests salvation can only come through "grace" (Acts 15:10). James says, "Instead we should write to them, telling them to abstain from food polluted by idols, from sexual immorality, from the meat of strangled animals and from blood." (Acts 15:20)[14] Hebrews can be viewed as a more expansive follow-up to these key passages, without their claimed authority (it was written later and its author is anonymous).

These passages are not as definitive as many claim. Acts was written by the author of the Gospel of Luke. In it the first person is used when describing events in Paul's life. Because of this and other evidence, Luke is traditionally held by Christians to have been a companion of Paul. An alternative, more sceptical, view holds that the author did not know Paul, in particular because Acts contradicts Paul's epistles about details of Paul's life. Either way, Luke and Acts foster an identifiably Pauline view of Christianity, with an emphasis on promoting Christianity to gentiles; and the account in Acts 15 serves Paul's agenda. Other books, for instance the Gospel of Matthew, have a noticeably different line. Since we have no writing that can be reliably attributed to Peter or James,[15] all we know of their views comes to us via a partisan of their opponent. A second problem is that, even if Acts 15 is accurate, it is ambiguous about exactly what Jewish Law was being abolished: it only explicitly does away with circumcision. Hebrews is similarly unclear on the bulk of Jewish Law.

And then we have Jesus's views as recorded in the Gospel of Matthew:

"Do not think that I have come to abolish the Law or the Prophets; I have not come to abolish them but to fulfil them. I tell you the truth, until heaven and earth disappear, not the smallest letter, not the least stroke of a pen, will by any means disappear from the Law until everything is accomplished. Anyone who breaks one of the least of these commandments and teaches others to do the same will be called least in the kingdom of heaven, but whoever practices and teaches these commands will be called great in the kingdom of heaven." (Matthew 5:17-19) [16]

In Matthew 7:21 Jesus says that "only he who does the will of my Father who is in heaven" will "enter the kingdom of heaven". John 5:29 has him promising eternal life only to "those who have done good".

On top of this – indeed, partly because of this – even the early "orthodox" church did not hold to the idea, which underpins the wholesale denial of Jewish Law, that salvation comes solely through faith rather than actions. A modern Christian work[17] cites numerous church fathers stating that following the Law was necessary to achieve salvation. Thus, for instance, Clement of Alexandria said that "whoever obtains [the truth] and distinguishes himself in good works shall gain the prize of everlasting life".

So the claims in Acts 15 and other commonly cited passages are hardly enough to justify Gumbel's moral/civil/ceremonial division, particularly when counterbalanced by Jesus's reported views. But in any case, no part of the New Testament actually explains which law falls into which category. Nor is the correct reinterpretation of "civil law" defined. Modern-day Christians have instead made these judgements for themselves, with much predictable disagreement.

It is hard not to conclude that the distinctions made are simply convenient. These days it is not convenient, for example, to keep the Sabbath holy, even though until relatively recently it was widely thought that businesses should not open on Sundays.[18] After all, the Ten Commandments instruct us to keep the Sabbath holy, and these commandments are "moral", unbreakable laws according to Gumbel. Elsewhere in the Old Testament the death penalty is imposed for breaking the Sabbath.[19] And yet we found Gumbel's own Holy Trinity Brompton's bookshop operating on a Sunday.

But then this perhaps isn't so surprising given that Gumbel also selectively ignores rules in the New Testament, which doesn't even purportedly fall into his classification scheme. We have already mentioned compulsory silence and hair covering for women in church. The author of 1 Peter says wives should not adorn themselves with jewellery and fine clothes (1 Peter 3:3). Christians should, according to Acts 15:20, eat only kosher meat. Jesus himself bans divorce except in the case of unfaithfulness (Matthew 5:31-32, 19:9). Why doesn't Alpha warn against divorce as well as (in *Searching Issues*) pre-marital sex? Presumably because it's easier to tell teenagers to be good than to force unhappy couples to remain together for the rest of their lives.

In any event, those who follow the rules of the Bible, whatever those may be, are said to be "transformed into the likeness" of God[20] and gain all kinds of spiritual rewards. Since the book is so useful, a plan for reading it is needed. After finding a solitary place (the manual quotes Mark,[21] although this actually talks about Jesus praying, not reading scripture), one should ask God to speak; then read, and ask oneself what it means and how it applies to one's own life. This had been a notably unsuccessful approach for me so far, but Mike did stress the openness to difficult questions – perhaps we would finally pin it down in the group.

The group's atmosphere this week was markedly different. Bill wasn't there, and the music teacher/tree surgeon couple were at the pub with Martin. Sandy seemed in good spirits, and was backed up by her husband Dr Phillip and the inevitable Anne. On the wavering side were Pete, Nadine and the ex-Catholic Belinda (she told us she'd just invested in a copy of Nicky Gumbel's *30 days*, a Bible reading programme).

Prompted by our comments in previous weeks, several people had actually read some of the more unpalatable parts of the Bible. Nadine hadn't been enjoying Leviticus.

"There's all this business on skin complaints – you're right." Sandy clucked in sympathy. "And all this stuff about periods!" they laughed together.

Anne had even held a competition with her youth group to find the silliest law in Leviticus. "The best one was… oh, I can't remember it… it's about aliens. I know it means foreigners, but it says aliens!"

"I once tried reading the Bible from the beginning," Pete cut in, "but I got bogged down in the middle of Genesis, I just couldn't handle all the endless begatting!"

Sandy agreed it was a tough read. She made it a point of honour to finish books but it was one of only three books that she had given up on.

Although the bizarre and unsavoury parts of the Bible were now at least partially out in the open, nobody saw any implications for belief in it as an infallible "manual for life". This was an axiom undefeatable by any absurdity it entailed.

I apologetically raised again the question of women's silence in church.

"The Bible was written in a different social context," said Nadine.

"But we were told we should live our life by it today, so some parts of it, at least, have relevance to our lives now. So which parts do we pick?" I asked.

Anne attempted an explanation. According to her, the all-important context was that ancient churches had had a problem with women chattering in the galleries. She provided no evidence for this claim, and in itself it does not negate Paul's commandment, just potentially explain it. The passage quite probably reflects the views of its time, but then that could also be said of biblical attitudes to homosexuality, and in that case Gumbel is clear that what might appear to be bigotry borne of ancient world ignorance must stand as God's will.

Besides, the demand for women's silence is hardly the only example of biblical sexism. In Genesis[22] God famously told women that, on account of Eve's crime in the Garden of Eden, they would bear the pain of childbirth and their husbands would rule over them. Sexist passages recur throughout the Old Testament. There are detailed rules on their role as the spoils of war;[23] they were deemed too unclean to fully partake in Jewish worship; and so on. And the New Testament carries an endorsement of the Old Testament's general anti-women position in 1 Timothy 2:11-14:

"Let a woman learn in silence with full submission. I permit no woman to teach or to have authority over a man; she is to keep silent. For Adam was formed first, then Eve; and Adam was not deceived, but the woman was deceived and became a transgressor."[24]

So implementing Paul's views on women speaking in church is hardly running against the tenor of the Bible.

I pointed to 1 Timothy 2. "I've never liked that passage," admitted Sandy, seeming a little embarrassed, but she supplied no reason beyond this for ignoring it.

"If the Bible is like a Highway Code for life, as Mike told us earlier, is it OK to ignore the parts that don't fit in with our plans?" I persisted.

It was, according to Pete: "We all speed a bit. What matters is our relationship with God." But ignoring God's rules surely could not help our relationship with Him. As Hebrews 10:26-27 says, "If we deliberately keep on sinning after we have received the knowledge of the truth, no sacrifice for sins is left, but only a fearful expectation of judgment and of raging fire that will consume the enemies of God."

"The thing is, I was reading Nicky Gumbel's book *Searching Issues*, and it says homosexuality is a sin because it's banned in the

Bible.[25] So again I'm not sure which parts of the Bible we follow and which we don't."

"I have trouble with this because I had a friend, and ever since he was three it was obvious..." admitted Sandy, who seemed a changed person from the previous time this subject had come up.

"I know it sounds bad, but I don't know anyone who's gay and... I mean, I have gay friends, but they're not part of the church. So it sounds bad but I just ignore the bits that don't apply to me, if you see what I mean," said Anne.

To some extent it seems reasonable to ignore the sections of the Bible that don't apply to oneself. To go with the Highway Code analogy, you probably wouldn't bother reading about towing a caravan if you didn't own one. But it did seem self-absorbed. In earlier sessions we were led to believe that God had infinite love. Yet he had apparently condemned an entire a class of people to hell for their sexuality. To my eyes the Bible was clear on the subject – they were doomed unless they repented of their sodomy. The shrugged replies seemed inadequate.

The divinely-breathed nature of the Bible raises another thorny problem: What about all the different versions of the Bible?

"I was wondering – it's another sort of academic question – about the different versions of the Bible. I mean, I understand the Bibles you're handing out have one set of books, and the Catholic Bible has some more, and the Orthodox more still. And I think the Ethiopian Church has yet another book in there. So I wonder how we know exactly which ones are the divinely-breathed ones."[26]

There was indifferent silence, just as there was on the related subject of "pseudoepigraphica" – books with false claims of authorship. It is striking that in his discussion of biblical authenticity Gumbel talks only about Jesus's life as revealed in the Gospels. Alpha gives no clue about the provenance or trustworthiness of the bulk of the rest of the New Testament, the Epistles, even though they form a crucial basis for Christian doctrine, and even though Gumbel frequently rests his arguments on their contents. This absence points to yet another inconsistency in his approach to scripture.

In *The Da Vinci Code: a response*, Gumbel inveighs against the apocryphal Nag Hammadi documents:

"Much of it is pseudoepigraphica which is at best a literary device, and at worst a fraud. For example, the gospel of Thomas claims to have been written by the apostle Thomas when it cannot possibly have been, as he had probably been dead for decades, if not centuries by the time they were written." [27]

The trouble is, if the scholarly consensus is accepted, the epistles to Timothy and Titus[28] employ "at best a literary device, and at worst a fraud", because in spite of their claims they weren't by Paul. Suspicion also commonly falls on Ephesians, Colossians and 2 Thessalonians. 2 Peter was almost certainly written by someone other than Peter, possibly as late as the second century CE.[29] Considering Peter is held to have died around 64 CE, Gumbel's dismissal of the Gospel of Thomas could largely be transferred to this epistle. 1 Peter's is also unlikely to be authentic. Its educated Greek style and references to the Septuagint, as well as its theological content, are implausible for an uneducated, Aramaic-speaking fisherman writing before 64 CE.[30]

When it comes to (Protestant) canonical books, though, Gumbel's standards evaporate. Without explanation he accepts Peter as author of 1 and 2 Peter,[31] and Paul as author of 1 and 2 Timothy and Ephesians.[32] He quotes them all, attributing the words to their traditional authors, unconcerned by possible fraud. I asked Bill in a later session if this was a problem. No, it wasn't, apparently, because the scholarly consensus on these books was wrong, as it frequently is according to fundamentalist Christians.

"The other thing is, I wonder about different translations. There's that example of Isaiah 7:14, where I think in the Bible you've given out, the New International Version (NIV), the Hebrew's been translated as "virgin", so it's saying the Messiah would be born of a virgin, and it's taken to be a prophecy of the virgin birth. But in my New Revised Standard Version it's translated as a 'young woman'. So again, I guess I wonder which is right."

This is an old point, but an important one that reveals something about Evangelicals' supposed reverence for the word of God, as well as the Bible's own lack of consistency. There is little question that the "conservative" NIV translation – the translation typically preferred by Evangelicals not irreversibly wedded to the even less accurate King

James translation – is wrong on this point. And it seems likely that the New International Version is preferred in part precisely *because* it is wrong on key details like this. It is "conservative" in the sense that it retains the errors of earlier translators, not because it accurately renders the original.

The Hebrew word in question is transliterated as "almah". It means "young woman" or "maiden", with no implication of virginity. Jewish translations of the text agree on this. Other Christian translations less beloved of fundamentalists agree.[33] The NIV agrees when the word is used elsewhere (e.g. Genesis 24:43). There is a different Hebrew word for virgin which is used in the Old Testament where that meaning is intended. Moreover, the passage in Isaiah is not obviously about God coming to earth. It is about King Ahaz of Judah, seven hundred years or so before Jesus, being reassured by the prophet Isaiah that his kingdom will not be taken over by foreign invaders. The word "almah" is preceded by a definite article ("ha'almah"), which implies that Isaiah is referring to a woman known to Ahaz. This last point was made by Thomas Paine in the eighteenth century but apparently still eludes Christian apologists.

In spite of all this, Christian evangelists persistently point to Isaiah 7:14 as an extraordinary prophecy fulfilled in a manner that can only point to God and biblical truth. Why? Presumably because the same mistake was made in Matthew 1:21, where the equivalent mistranslation into Greek fed the same unwarranted interpretation. With Matthew making so much of Isaiah's supposed prediction, "Bible-believing" Christians have little choice but to follow suit. Pushing this false view was easier back when the King James Edition held sway. Nowadays they have to hand out the NIV and hope, no doubt with good reason, that most of the audience will never look beyond what it and credulous apologetics say on the subject. This reliance on ideologically-dictated translations is commonly maintained in concert with loud insistence that the Bible is infallible.

But this didn't matter to the group. Will made vague noises about differences of opinion until Pete broke in with a more reassuring Bible tale. He'd been pestered by his wife to write a letter to put in a time capsule for his infant daughter. Having just read *Mere Christianity* by C.S.Lewis he'd chosen to include a verse from the Bible. Initially, he'd wanted to include Psalm 23.

"You know the 'even though I walk through the valley of the shadow of death' one? But then I thought, I'll just let the Bible fall open, and take something from there. And do you know? It fell open at Psalm 23!"

I wanted to suggest that maybe this was because he'd been looking at that passage earlier. Instead I said, "You're lucky it wasn't Leviticus!" He laughed. The obscenities and absurdities, although acknowledged, had no implications for his faith. If he'd been just a little less lucky, the Bible might have fallen open at Psalm 137, another famous one ("By the rivers of Babylon…"). It goes on to say how wonderful it would be to smash Babylonian babies against rocks.[34]

So what could we conclude? The Alpha course teaches that the Bible is "God's rule book" and a "manual for life", but the Christians we met there simply ignored the parts they didn't feel comfortable with. Their only justification was the weak, selective argument that an ill-defined set of rules are enshrouded in "historical context". But a good Alpha student must nevertheless keep in mind that the text was divinely-breathed and is pretty much infallible – even the parts that lie about who wrote them, and even if Christians can't agree on which books this applies to or how to translate them. How should we read the Bible? We should read whichever parts we like and forget the rest, all the while maintaining that it is the ultimate guide to life.

Notes

1. *Questions of Life,* p.68-70.
2. Ibid., p.70.
3. See Appendix C for what following this manual strictly entails.
4. *Questions of Life,* p.75.
5. Ibid., p.73.
6. Ibid., p.75.
7. 2 Timothy 3:16: "All Scripture is God-breathed and is useful for teaching, rebuking, correcting and training in righteousness".
8. In other words, the Bible was divinely inspired because the people who wrote it said it was. The same argument could be made for any text making the same sort of claims, although Christians only apply it to the Bible. Note also that if 2 Timothy, as modern scholarship suggests, was not actually written by its purported author then the words claiming their origin with God were written by an imposter.
9. *Questions of Life,* p.74.

10. Ibid., p.71. "…for him [Jesus], what the scriptures said God said (Mark 7:5-13). If Jesus is our Lord, our attitude to the Scriptures should be the same as his".

11. Ibid., p.73. Here Gumbel ingeniously suggests that, because suffering is impossible to reconcile with God's goodliness, yet Christians somehow manage to ignore this, we should persevere with these "difficult" passages. So because Christians already accept some contradictions, this should be taken as inspiration to accept more contradictions.

12. *Challenging Lifestyle*, p.227-228.

13. Ehrman, B.D. (2005). *Lost Christianities: The Battles for Scripture and the Faiths We Never Knew*. OUP.

14. Note that this is only one of the versions of Acts 15:20. Other versions retain a different array of Jewish practices, further confusing the issue.

15. The Epistle of James in the form we have it was almost certainly not written by the James referred to in Acts 15. The two epistles of Peter were, similarly, almost certainly not written by Peter. The words attributed to James in Acts 15 are also unlikely to be authentic, as they have him quoting the Greek version of the Old Testament.

16. Although Jesus's sermon in Luke 6 has many similarities with Matthew 5's Sermon the Mount, this passage, or anything like it, is notably absent. This is suggestive of Luke's agenda mentioned above.

17. David, W. (1999). *Will the Real Heretics Please Stand Up* (3rd Ed), Scroll Publishing Company, chapter 6.

18. There is a separate issue of the *day* of the Sabbath: without any scriptural justification it switched from Saturday to Sunday. Seventh Day Adventists, who consider themselves Christian, observe the Sabbath on Saturday.

19. Exodus 31:14-15, Numbers 15:32-34. Christians tend to cite some New Testament passages in favour of breaking the Sabbath (e.g. Colossians 2:16, Galatians 4:8-11). These passages are far vaguer than the Old Testament ones they allegedly negate, and there are comparably non-specific New Testament passages pointing in the other direction. In any case, Gumbel cannot push this interpretation without contradicting his claim about the Ten Commandments being unbreakable "moral laws".

20. 2 Corinthians 3:18: "And all of us, with unveiled faces, seeing the glory of the Lord as though reflected in a mirror, are being transformed into the same image from one degree of glory to another".

21. Mark 1:35: "In the morning, while it was still very dark, [Jesus] got up and went out to a deserted place, and there he prayed."

22. Genesis 3:16: "To the woman he said, 'I will greatly increase your pains in childbearing; with pain you will give birth to children. Your desire will be for your husband, and he will rule over you.'"

23. Deuteronomy 21:10-13 assures Jewish victors that they can take beautiful female prisoners as their wives, provided they first shave their heads, cut their nails, and throw their clothes away. The presumption is that the captive's parents have been killed, so sex is banned for month while they are mourned.

24. Ephesians 5:22-24 also enjoins: "Wives, submit to your husbands as to the Lord… as the church submits to Christ, so also wives should submit to their husbands in everything."

25. See *Searching Issues,* p.72. See also Chapter 4.

26. There are several apparently Christian texts that were excluded from the Bible by the early church. These include the Gnostic texts gathered in the Nag Hammadi library, which include extra gospels and even a book claiming to be Confucius-style sayings of Jesus.

27. *The Da Vinci Code: a response,* p.11.

28. *TNOAB,* New Testament, page 349, says, "most scholars today regard them as pseudoepigraphical".

29. *TNOAB* says "[t]here is little historical or literary evidence to connect the author of [2 Peter] either to Simon Peter or to the author of 1 Peter… The letter was probably written from Rome around the end of the first century CE or the beginning of the second." (New Testament, p.401)

30. In Acts 4:13 Peter is described as "agrammatoi" (αγραμματοι), meaning "uneducated" or "illiterate". *TNOAB* says "most critical scholars interpret the document as a letter from the last decade of the first century CE, written in Peter's name in order to claim that its teaching represented the apostolic faith".

31. *Questions of Life,* p.43 & 72.

32. *Searching Issues,* p.26, *Questions of Life,* p.71 & 215.

33. E.g. the Bible in Basic English, the New English Bible, New English Translation Bible, the New Jerusalem Bible and the Revised Standard Version.

34. Psalm 137:8-9: "O Daughter of Babylon, doomed to destruction, happy is he who repays you for what you have done to us- he who seizes your infants and dashes them against the rocks."

CHAPTER 7

A Chinwag with God

The "How Should I Pray?" session began quietly. Our late arrival meant the Christian dinner companions usually on standby weren't available. It took until the coffee and cake phase for Anne to appear, and her main preoccupation was her mother, who didn't like her going drinking after Alpha sessions.

Soon we were being urged, accompanied by inspirational music, to leave the tables and sit down for Tom's talk. Unfortunately this was the first week lacking the full comic pairing. Tom delivered a warm-up routine anyway. Mike, we were told, had once been attacked by a bear, whereupon he'd cried out to God. Suddenly time had frozen, the river had stopped flowing, and he'd taken the moment to ask for help: "Please God, I know it's wrong to kill this bear, so could you make him a Christian? A Christian bear wouldn't kill a clergyman." God had granted his wish but – aha! – poor Mike heard the bear say, "Thank you dear Lord for what I am about to receive…"

According to Tom, prayer is a crucial part of every Christian's life, the mould being set by Jesus himself, who prayed regularly to God. Of course, we know from the doctrine of the Trinity that Jesus's prayer was directed at himself, so he was in the fortunate position of deciding whether to answer his own prayers. Results for average mortals are more variable. Nevertheless, this one-sided conversation is the "most important activity of our lives". It develops the all-important relationship with God, and for extra goodness it involves all three members of the Trinity. Gumbel reveals that when we pray it is to God in heaven, although we "have no right in ourselves to come to God" and have to pray "through" Jesus or "in his name". Bafflingly, at the same time as we pray, God is simultaneously "praying through us by his Spirit".[1] The arrangement is as logical and transparent as the idea of the Trinity itself.

Tom next addressed a common objection to prayer: If God is omniscient and knows what we're going to ask for, then why ask at all? Part of the answer is that, because God lives in the "eternal present", he hears all prayers simultaneously, which means they can be retroactive, among other things. Furthermore, God "has all eternity to answer the split second prayer of a driver who is about to crash". According to one writer quoted by Gumbel, God "can appropriate a prayer from next week, and attach it to an event a month ago." Sci-fi B-movie paradoxes aside, does prayer work in a straightforward case, where no violation of the space-time continuum is required? Does the power of prayer enhance the lives of Christians on average? This, after all, is what many Christians claim. If God were more likely to answer the prayers of Christians then surely it would be possible to identify a tendency for Christians to have better luck and health and so on.

Here Gumbel wants to have it both ways.[2] He says it is "not possible to prove Christianity on the basis of answers to prayer because they can always be explained away, by cynics, as coincidences". Then he asserts that "the cumulative effect of answered prayer reinforces our faith in God" and reveals the existence of his "prayer diary", which he says shows that "day after day…God has answered my prayers." He presents only anecdotal and subjective evidence, and yet makes the strong statement: "Every Christian knows… that God answers prayer."

The subject does not want for study. Back in the 19th Century, the statistician Francis Galton famously noted that members of the British royal family should be far fitter than the rest of the population, as church congregations across the country were praying for them every Sunday. He demonstrated that there was no statistical difference between them and the rest of the population. More recently, a high profile study was conducted on the effects of prayer on coronary bypass patients.[3] 1,800 patients were randomly allocated to one of three groups. One group knew they were being prayed for by a team of Christian intercessors; one was being prayed for but were not aware of it; and one was not being prayed for at all. The results showed that patients who were prayed for were no more likely to improve than the others. Worse, the patients who knew they were being prayed for suffered more complications than those who were unaware. Finally, it is only fit to mention that a recent meta-analysis of 14 intercessory prayer studies found no discernible effect of prayer and recommended that all funding for this line of research be stopped.[4]

In spite of all this, many Christians still insist that there is scientific evidence for healing prayer. When not simply anecdotal, this tends to centre on dubious cherry-picked results, in particular those of an oft-cited study[5] in which 6 out of 26 patients showed improvements when they were prayed for. However, even many scientists holding Christian beliefs have now rejected this study, as on important outcomes such as mortality and length of hospital stay there was no difference between those prayed for and those not prayed for. Another "successful" prayer study was published in 2001, where Christian prayer appeared to increase the chances of successful in-vitro fertilisation by somewhere in the region of 25%.[6][7] The study was embroiled in controversy when one author, Daniel Wirth, was found guilty of large-scale fraud. The other two authors subsequently distanced themselves from the project, with one admitting that he had only provided "editorial assistance" a year after the study was supposed to have taken place.

Under certain assumptions, then, prayer as a healing force has been tested and has been found deficient. But resort can always be made to hazy terminology and godly caprice to throw out these assumptions, as Gumbel did with talk of retrospective prayer. If prayer can affect anything at any time in any way then of course nothing about it can be meaningfully tested.

For instance, there is the problem of "background prayer". Many patients are already being prayed for by relatives and their communities. Congregations and individuals also commonly offer blanket prayers aimed at entire classes of people, such as everyone in the world with the same type of illness. It is close to impossible, therefore, to know the amount of prayer directed at a test subject. Since Christians regularly act as if the quantity of their prayer influences God, this alone is a major difficulty with scientific trials. There is also the possibility of outsiders praying for these studies not to work. As one researcher commented, "complete strangers… can well entreat God in their prayers to confound the studies. Indeed, we could even plead with God to mess up the studies retroactively! Strangers who… think that it is a bad idea to use randomised control studies to study the healing power of prayer could well beg God to 'put those scientists in their place'… No matter what the results, somebody's prayers will have been answered".[8]

In an attempt to avoid some of these confounds, researchers have instead concentrated on non-conscious entities such as plants and cells, but there again we find a lack of evidence to support the case that prayer works. To take one example, a study of the effects of prayer on in vitro cancer cells revealed absolutely no effect of prayer on the cells.[9] The results are similar in numerous experiments with people praying for seeds to grow. In fact we found only one study that appeared to show some effect of supernatural entreaty on non-conscious entities. "Treated" lettuces were said to have reached a larger size and resisted slug attack.[10] Unfortunately the intercessor in this case was a spiritualist faith healer. We were later warned about this type of "New Age" practitioner as a vessel of demonic power.[11] This illustrates yet another difficulty: In a world rife with evil countervailing supernatural forces, how would anyone know which miraculous interventions were godly?

Fundamentally, an answered prayer as defined by Evangelical Christians is too hazy a concept to be tested for. With a god given to whimsical violation of physical laws, what scientific experiment can conclude anything? Predictably, certain Christian apologists have latched onto this notion as a shield against scrutiny, as we found when talking to Bill on the subject (see chapter 14). Just as predictably, they do not accept that this technique of eliminating even the possibility of scientific proof renders meaningless the empirical claims that they make on prayer's behalf. Gumbel displays precisely this combination.

He also attaches unwarranted significance to anecdotal evidence. This is by definition scientifically irrelevant, but it is perhaps worth considering just one example of how apparently inexplicable healings live on as propaganda tools regardless of supporting evidence. A critical account of Charismatic Christianity, *Charismania*,[12] relates how prolific author Jennifer Rees Larcombe was apparently struck down by crippling viral encephalitis and, after much suffering, healed when prayed for by a young woman she met at a Christian meeting. She related the experience in a book called *Unexpected Healing*, and was featured on the cover of *Renewal* magazine holding her wheelchair over her head. According to *Charismania*, it subsequently emerged that she had in fact never been diagnosed with viral encephalitis and that physical tests had shown her to be normal. This has not restricted her writing since. In subsequent years Rees Larcombe has reiterated her "miraculous" story multiple times, for instance in 2006's *Journey into God's Heart: The True Story of a Life of Faith*. Evangelicals continue to parrot her claims as if medical records are a nitpicking refuge of the pathologically ungodly.[13] Her publisher's website describes her as "one of the world's most-loved Christian teachers and writers".

In summary, if there were compelling statistically significant evidence of healing prayer's efficacy then one would expect to find it in Gumbel's books (among many others), but he presents none. Instead he retreats into anecdote and vagueness, if not self-contradiction, while peddling a definition of an answered prayer so ductile that it allows an infinite set of possible explanations for any given sequence of events and related prayers, destroying the possibility of a rigorous test. In practice, as with other elements of the Alpha doctrine supposedly founded on empirical evidence, the real justification appears to be to subjective faith. It's just that Gumbel can't bring himself to admit this.

Unsurprisingly, these conclusions are not popular with fundamentalist Christians, and several websites have grotesquely misrepresented the results of prayer experiments in an attempt to prove that prayer works and mislead the uninformed. And even if they admit the failure of these studies, healing prayer advocates usually reject the whole concept of scientific investigation of prayer. God, they say, would never allow the effects of prayer to be measured in such a way, and will only answer prayers offered up for the right reasons (we found this in our group – see chapter 14). Richard Dawkins even quotes one eminent theologian as suggesting that prayer experiments don't work because "too much [evidence] might not be good for us".[14]

Instead of showing that prayer actually works at all, Tom moved straight to why prayers aren't *always* answered. He offered the cautionary story of Nicky Gumbel's squash partner, a thoroughly nice man with six children, who nonetheless dropped dead during a game. No amount of prayer had resurrected him, and God's decision seemed inexplicable. But that hadn't put off Gumbel, who decided he could make a choice of trusting God or not. He'd decided to trust him, although it isn't clear why, given that his behaviour in this case seems incompatible with a loving nature, and his loving nature was presented as a reason to trust him.

Predictably enough, if there *is* blame to be found in Alpha world for unanswered prayer, it lies with us, not God. Tom told us about the various possibilities given in the Bible. One is unconfessed sin or disobedience toward God, which can create a "barrier" in our relationship. Or the motive behind the prayer might be wrong – if we simply pray for material goods, God is unlikely to comply. Lastly, God will not grant us things that are not good for us ("you wouldn't give a carving knife to a three year old just because she asked for it"), even if they appear to be so in the short term. This seems fair, but what about the good things that would manifestly help humanity, such as food for the starving? The fall back explanation was that we don't understand God's purpose. Even if God seems thoroughly capricious, even cruel, we should trust him because he loves us, and he always does things for our own good.

There is, then, a basically incomprehensible conception of "love" being used. In spite of much evidence in and outside the Bible that God is not "loving" in the sense usually understood by humans, we are still urged to regard him as such – and even more strangely, to infer from this that he will act in a loving fashion in terms that we do understand. When he's slaughtering millions via natural disasters, or liquidating squash-playing family men, or failing to cure a blameless cancer sufferer, he is "loving" in an ineffable divine sense beyond the reach of human understanding. When he does intervene against human suffering, in his arbitrary and scientifically undetectable manner, he's "loving" in a more recognizable sense. Both senses are invoked when convenient, and on account of some combination of them we are advised to feel great joy.

The rest of the talk focused on practical questions of where to pray and what to say, as ever backed up with a stream of Bible quotes. The only part that stuck in my mind was Tom urging us that anywhere would do for prayer, including the toilet.

Bill began the discussion with the usual question, "So, what did everyone think of it?" His eyes settled on Pete.

"There's not much to talk about really," Pete reckoned. "Since you're allowed to ask for pretty much anything, in pretty much any way, what is there to worry about?"

Bill looked for another response and settled on Wilma, who as usual looked flustered and embarrassed: "It was nice... yeah nice... nothing controversial"

"What about people's own experiences with prayer?" asked Bill.

Again he got non-committal replies, apart from Nadine the big-haired Armenian, who was excited because someone had suggested to her the idea that reading the Bible was a form of prayer.

"Can I ask what you pray about?" Malc asked Bill.

"It doesn't have to be anything personal" Bill said. His prayers ranged from personal matters to world peace, all of which he noted down in his own Gumbel-inspired prayer diary. He liked to tick off prayers in his diary that had been answered.

"I pray for strength," Belinda told us, and immediately launched into a chattering monologue about Catholic prayer. The conversation then meandered onto whether praying out loud was necessary. The consensus was that it wasn't, although Bill was concerned about one's mind wandering during silent prayer.

This prompted Malc to ask, "If thinking prayers is praying, why specifically pray at all? Is there a difference between merely thinking about something and praying?"

According to Bill it had to be "directed thought" which was needed to "build a relationship with God".

"I was wondering if God answers non-Christians' prayers," I told Bill.

He initially didn't seem keen to commit to an answer, but eventually decided that yes, God would answer their prayers.

"Who do you mean?" Nadine asked me, sounding suspicious.

"Well, for instance, do Mormons' prayers get answered?"

"I thought they were Christians..."

"Well my understanding is they're regarded as heretical, but I wouldn't get too fixated on Mormons. I'm wondering about any other religions, say Islam... or Buddhism – do they get their prayers answered?"

"I was a Buddhist for six months," Nadine giggled, "and you know it's all chanting – the complete opposite of Christianity, they'll chant for a new car or whatever!" When I quizzed her about it later she told me she couldn't really speak about other religions because she'd be guilty of breaking religious hatred laws.

Anne had a confession: "It sounds stupid, but I actually prayed for a car… I needed it for youth work… and I prayed for a car, and I got a Peugeot 205, and it lasted just long enough – I needed it for nine months – and then it blew up on the motorway."

I felt we were straying from the point. "Right… um, I'm still wondering if God answers Christians' prayers more than non-Christians' ones though? I'm thinking of the bit in the Alpha manual where it says disobedience can block prayer from succeeding[15] – I'm assuming non-Christians are generally more disobedient when it comes to God's laws."

Bill leant forward, and asked me, "What is your position here? Where are you coming from?" Bringing up the subject of other religions never seemed popular in the discussion group – it complicated things.

"Well, I'm coming from a position of doubt. I don't know what to believe, and different religions say different things. So I'm wondering which is the right one."

"Well, God is all-merciful, so I think he does answer their prayers, yes."[16]

"So there's no benefit in being Christian when it comes to prayer?"

"I think that would be between you and God," said Bill, grinning.

"Right… well I guess I have different idea of God. I mean, he doesn't seem that merciful to non-believers. The verse in the manual,[17] where Nicky Gumbel says people shouldn't go to astrologers… that same verse says non-believers will be cast into a fiery lake of sulphur. Or there's Mark 16:16…"[18]

Bill scrambled for his Bible. "What does that say?"

"It says people who haven't been baptised will not be saved."

Bill picked on the distinction between the unbeliever and the un-baptised, so I raised another passage in John,[19] which explicitly says that the unbeliever is condemned. His response was the example of a Roman centurion who saw a vision from God.[20] I pointed out that the followers of Baal specifically did not have their prayers answered during a showdown with Yahweh's followers,[21] but it was impossible to dislodge Bill's faith in universal mercy. His arguments seemed to imply a contradictory Bible, or at least a Bible incapable of clearly resolving this fundamental question.

Anne had a novel take on the terms of our debate: "Can I jump in there? It might be completely wrong… but I think unbelievers are people who haven't heard of Christianity." Pointing out that there was no biblical basis for this interpretation was met with indifferent silence.

"Well that was a bit of a conversation killer!" exclaimed Pete before launching into what he thought could prevent prayer working. It was doing what you thought was wrong. This set off yet another discussion on the definition of sin and whether certain rules of the Bible should be followed. We seemed to be going backwards.

I had wanted to ask about the difficulty of proving prayer's effect. If we could validate prayer by a scientific comparison of prayer diaries I felt I might finally have a compelling reason to believe in the Bible. However, I didn't get the chance before our session ended and it was time to join Pete at the pub.

When we arrived Elspeth was deep in conversation with some other Christian women. They were discussing the awful possibility that there were fleas in the armchairs. Gordon told us a little more about the path to becoming a Christian ninja, although we learned nothing about the supernatural happenings that he had witnessed. Still, he seemed less distrustful than the others, who appeared to write us off as soon as I made the mistake of asking what "HTB" stood for (in the trade this is shorthand for Holy Trinity Brompton, the fount of the Alpha Course).

Once Pete had appeared and introduced his brother-in-law, he told us a little about his background. He'd arrived in Britain and immediately been conned into a low-paid furniture delivery job. Since then he had been impressed by British people's politeness, having previously assumed they would "step over a dead body". He was keen to convey his changing impressions of me: "To be honest Stuart, at first I thought you were just a gimmick, someone who just turned up to spring things on people." But now he'd decided I was sincere. He was baffled by our questioning because he'd always thought he was a cynic, and here we were asking "all sorts of questions" he'd "never thought about". It seemed a signature attribute of an Alpha attendee to have never seriously questioned Christianity, but he did say that he felt they were important questions.

"Would you", he wondered, "do another Alpha Course if you aren't satisfied at the end of this one?" Or would I perhaps investigate another religion? In fact he seemed to think it was my duty to look at other religions if I was rejecting Christianity, as if the presumption must be in favour of Christianity until dislodged by superior religious claims.

Pete's companions were distinctly less friendly, sitting with their Alpha manuals proudly displayed and largely restricting their conversation to their co-religionists. I formed the strong impression that fitting in among such people would require a fairly complete adoption of their beliefs. Pete surely had little choice.

Notes

1. *Questions of Life*, p.83-90.
2. Ibid., p.88.
3. Benson, H., Dusek, J., Sherwood, J., Lam, P., Bethea, C., Carpenter, W., Levitsky, J., Hill, P., Clem Jr, D., & Jain, M. (1997). *American Heart Journal*, 151 (4), 934-942.
4. Masters, S. K., Spielmans, G. I. & Goodson, J. T. (2006). Are there demonstrable effects of distant intercessory prayer? A meta-analytic review. *Annals of Behavioural Medicine*, 32(1), 21-26.
5. Byrd, R. (1988). Positive Therapeutic Effects of Intercessory Prayer in a Coronary Care Unit Population. *Southern Medical Journal*, 81(7), 826-829.
6. Cha, K.Y., Wirth, D.P. & Lobo, R.A. (2001). Does prayer influence the success of in vitro fertilisation-embryo transfer? Report of a masked, randomised trial. *Journal of Reproductive Medicine*, 46(9), 781-787.
7. Also discussed in: Grant, J. (2008). *Corrupted science: fraud, ideology and politics in science*. Facts, Figures and Fun, UK.
8. Turner, D. (2006). Just another drug? A philosophical assessment of randomised controlled studies on intercessory prayer. *Journal of Medical Ethics*, 32, 487-490.
9. Zachariae, R., Hoggard, L., Zachariae, C., Vaeth, M., Bang, B., & Skov, L. (2005). The effect of spiritual healing on *in vitro* tumour cell proliferation and viability – an experimental study. *British Journal of Cancer*, 93, 538-543.
10. Roney-Dougal, S.M., & Solfvin, J. (2003). Field study of an enhancement effect on lettuce seeds: a replication study. *Journal of Parapsychology*, 67(2), 279-297.

11. See Chapter 11.
12. Howard, R. (1997). *Charismania*. Mowbray, London.
13. As just one example of the many uncritical mentions on the Internet, the Fellowship of Independent Evangelical Churches spring 2007 women's newsletter reviewed *Journey into God's Heart*, saying, "Confined to a wheelchair for eight years as a result of encephalitis, she was undeniably miraculously healed… [S]he is very honest in hers and her families' struggles to adjust to her health."
14. Dawkins, R. (2006). *The God Delusion*. Bantam Press, London.
15. *Questions of Life,* p.89.
16. On page 88 of *Questions of Life* Gumbel actually says God "sometimes… graciously answers the prayer of an unbeliever" but it is implied that this is very unusual.
17. Revelation 21:8: "But the cowardly, the unbelieving, the vile, the murderers, the sexually immoral… – their place will be in the fiery lake of burning sulphur. This is the second death."
18. Mark 16:16: "Whoever believes and is baptised will be saved, but whoever does not believe will be condemned." Most scholars believe Mark 16:9-17 was not in the original version of Mark, so if Christians are prepared to discard that part they could avoid explaining away Mark 16:16. However, as should be clear, the sentiment is expressed elsewhere in the Bible
19. John 3:18: "Whoever believes in him is not condemned, but whoever does not believe stands condemned already…."
20. See Acts 10-11.
21. See 1 Kings 18.

CHAPTER 8

Long, wide… and deep

"I can't really tell you what will happen, but trust me you won't believe it!" So went the buzz about the next part of the course, the Holy Spirit Weekend (or day in our case). For the last few weeks the excitement had been building. The organizers had been dropping hints and nodding at rumours. If nothing else in the Alpha Course was convincing, this, we were told, was sure to be.

Back before the course started, Jonathan Aitken had located his turning point in this weekend. At the Alpha Supper, a convert from last year had been brought on-stage to tell us how she'd been won over during the weekend session. We had been told that "amazing" things would happen when attendees were "filled with the Holy Spirit". We were warned that it would be an emotional session: previous Holy Spirit Weekends had been replete with screaming, swooning, crying and speaking in tongues. Gumbel sets great store by the Holy Spirit experience, devoting three entire chapters of *Questions of Life* to it.

In this he was influenced by the "Toronto Blessing", where in 1994 congregationists at Toronto Airport Church responded to manifestations of the Holy Spirit by entering "a trance-like state, fall[ing] to the floor shaking, laughing, shouting – or even making animal noises". Various fools for Christ barked like dogs, roared like lions, and – appropriately perhaps – emitted cuckoo clock noises. Alongside zoo keeping, the Holy Spirit also moonlighted as a dentist, with "over 50 people… testifying to having received what appeared to be gold or bright silver fillings or crowns, which they believed had supernaturally appeared in their mouths after receiving prayer". The miracle has since repeated in, of all places, Croydon.[1]

We arrived late, missing Mike's first amusing story, but not much of the first talk: "Who is the Holy Spirit?" The message was that other Christians frequently lack full appreciation of this entity. A smattering of Biblical references showed what the Spirit could do. In Exodus[2] he was responsible for a man named Bezalel's artistic work, although the point was weakened when Mike stressed that one could be an ungodly artist too – the Holy Spirit "just helps out a bit from time to time". In Judges the Holy Spirit granted leadership to Gideon.[3] The New Testament also has various miraculous happenings attributed to the Holy Spirit. The most important, of course, was the Pentecostal intercession of the Spirit,[4] where the disciples were given the amazing ability to speak any language.

The talk aimed to convince attendees that they were going to be personally filled with a manifestation of God. The justification relied on questionable readings of Old Testament books written before the notion of the Christian Holy Spirit existed,[5] and a very literal interpretation of New Testament stories. The point of the exercise was, it seemed, to sidestep the lack of hard evidence for Christianity. A waverer not convinced by the historical evidence for Jesus's divinity might take instead the evidence of a personal spiritual experience.

After a short coffee and cakes interval we were on to a new talk: "What does the Holy Spirit do?" It began with another joke from Tom. This time there wasn't even a punch-line – it just set up various members of the church, only some of whose names were familiar to the non-devotee, as being more or less godly according to which vehicle they were rewarded with in heaven. The tittering reached a crescendo when Bill, who was operating the projector, flashed up a message saying Tom's jokes weren't very good.

The talk itself was vague. I was already getting the feeling that they were stretching insubstantial material too far. For instance, apparently the Holy Spirit helps us pray and enables us to understand God's word in some unspecified way – he "keeps us going". The Spirit also hands over gifts. Malcolm Muggeridge, influential in promoting Mother Theresa in the early days (he suggested a divine light had aided a cameraman filming her work[6]), described the effect of the Spirit as a "rapture". It allows Christians to "witness for Christ", and gives them power for his service.[7]

Following these hazy declarations, we decamped to the vestry for our only discussion of the day. Lunch immediately followed so, as ever, there wasn't a great deal of time to pin things down. Only Bill, Sandy, Belinda, Pete and Nadine were present.

Bill wanted us to relate personal emotional experiences, but seemingly none of the waverers had had a remarkable experience with the Holy Spirit, so he filled time by telling us about his faith transition. He'd spent a lot of time "intellectually" studying Christianity, but hadn't achieved a "full faith". Then, after he had "thrown down the gauntlet", he had experienced an apparently conclusive "amazing joy".

Sandy had a more dramatic tale. After a bereavement she had detected an extraordinary calming presence in the room where her family were gathered. Most remarkably, the cats had stopped purring. As she related this, a joyous smile appeared on her face. Initially frightened by the experience, she had spoken to a vicar who gave her a Bible and suggested that she had just witnessed the presence of God. "The most amazing thing was the cats," she stressed again.

I felt bound to ask about the explanations given for these rapturous encounters. "I was just wondering… I've no doubt people have had these feelings of joy and so on, but I wonder how we know what the explanation is. We're told these experiences are a reason to believe in the Bible, but we're using the Bible to interpret them, so I'm thinking maybe there's some circularity there."

Bill sat studiously, giving no sign of comprehension.

"I mean, people in other contexts have spiritual experiences, and they interpret them differently, not using the Bible. We use the Bible here, so we see the Holy Spirit in these things, but how do we know it's the right source to use when interpreting them?"

Bill gave his usual shrug. "Does anyone have an answer to that?" he asked the room, finally looking towards Pete.

"Ah, well I'm afraid you lost me about halfway through there!" he replied.

"I'm just wondering about all the other spiritual experiences around the world. People interpret them in a way that fits their background. So if you are from a Buddhist country you are more likely to interpret it from a Buddhist perspective. So how do we know the Bible is the right way to interpret spiritual experiences here?"

"It's all the same god, though," said Nadine, irritated. She still hadn't grasped that this was explicitly not the message of the Alpha Course. Not wanting to dominate the discussion I left it there.

Bill and Pete then talked at length about the "journey" to Christianity – was it preordained? This seemed to presuppose that there was a Christian god doing the ordaining, so wasn't very interesting to someone not already converted.

Belinda seemed keen to equate the journey with her move from an unfriendly Catholic church to this far friendlier Anglican one. "I felt no warmth there. You know, when I first came here for the Jonathan Aitken talk I was really worried – you know, I didn't know anyone – who was I going to sit with? But you know, everybody was SO friendly," she happily told us, as if religious convictions should derive from the friendliness of their promoters.

Eventually I felt I had to mention something about this "journey", because Bill kept implying that whatever religious history one might have, Christianity was the natural destination.

"I was thinking – about this talk of journeys – that people don't always move towards Christianity. My grandmother, who's ninety, went to church for, well, until a couple of years ago. Now she's a Buddhist. So I don't think it's likely her journey will end up with Christianity."

Bill was unimpressed. "Well obviously individual churches can fail people," he sternly told me. So someone couldn't turn away from Christianity after rigorously evaluating rival religious claims. It could only be because they hadn't had the Lord explained to them sufficiently well, or in a friendly enough fashion.

Unfortunately the discussion stopped then for lunch in the concrete church hall. After walking down with Bill, chatting about air shows and helicopters, I collected my unholy combination of pumpkin soup and rubbery vegeburger. We sat in a circle on plastic chairs and ate. Nadine was on my left, but didn't seem especially keen on talking at first, so I listened in on the discussion about Christianity in the armed forces that Pete, Malc and Bill were having. Both Bill, who had been in the Territorial Army and the RAF, and Pete, who'd done eighteen months' national service in South Africa, seemed to think that the military was sadly lacking in Christianity. Bill was keen to stress its importance for combating immoral behaviour – women and drinking were particular problems.

I talked to Nadine, who told me she had been born in Istanbul before moving with her parents to Glasgow. Every summer they would drive all the way back to Turkey when all she wanted was to go to Butlins like her friends. She said she used to go to an Armenian church but had no idea what was going on because she didn't actually speak Armenian. Suddenly her ignorance of the Bible made sense, if for forty years she had been hearing the Good Word in a foreign language. The friendly, apparently open, discussion of Alpha would surely seem far preferable to incomprehensible ritualistic worship.

After the lengthy morning build-up we joined the afternoon session with great anticipation. This was when the "amazing" stuff we had heard about was supposed to happen. The talk, titled "How can I be filled with the Holy Spirit?", was sure to tell us how to achieve it. I was waiting to witness someone speaking in tongues, but before this information could be divulged we had to wade through some inspiring guitar ensemble-backed music, with these the only lyrics:

Open the eyes of my heart Lord,
Open the eyes of my heart,
I want to see you,
I want to see you (x2)

This went round and round for a short eternity, as the band leader rapped on the microphone: "Open… your heart… let the Lord in." In response, a girl in the next row with a large crucifix tattoo on her back kicked off her shoes, threw her hands in the air, started swaying with her eyes closed, mouthing the words to the song with a look of ecstasy on her face. After this, Mike's humorous anecdotes were unexpectedly welcome (they involved "ugly sticks", bus drivers and hide-and-seek phone calls).

Mike first focused on the overwhelming power of the Holy Spirit to convert unbelievers, in particular St Paul. He reminded us that Paul had instigated the first stoning to death of a Christian martyr, and had "set about destroying the church", dragging "men and women off to prison". However, after encountering Jesus on the road to Damascus he had been filled with the Holy Spirit and immediately become a zealous

Christian convert.[8] Later, Paul laid his hands on some "uninformed" Ephesians who were then filled with the Holy Spirit and "began speaking in tongues and prophesising".[9] More modern conversions, while less remarkable, were also attributed to the Spirit's works.

"Some people who are not Christians, even anti-Christians, become powerful advocates," Mike said. He admitted that his only example, Jonathan Aitken, provoked considerable scepticism. "People ask, 'is it a real conversion?', but actually I believe here is a man who is soundly converted." Oddly, Aitken's "sound" conversion came with an unwillingness to clarify his alleged role in corrupt arms deals and prostitute procurement. Having admitted only perjury, he was said to have left those he had unsuccessfully sued for libel with huge legal bills. And then there was his aborted bid to re-enter politics. Would he have remained so committed to Alpha if he had been able to renew his political career?

But Mike didn't linger. Instead he issued a pre-emptive attack on wariness of public emotion. He warned of the dangers of a lack of emotion in our relationship with God, and encouraged us to practise "spontaneous praise". He briefly admitted that there was a danger of "emotionalism" – an excess of emotion – but his attitude was overwhelmingly positive. Then he launched into what seemed to be a veiled attack on the non-Charismatic wing of Christianity, saying that as a trainee preacher he had toured too many "cold" churches, lacking the "warmth or love" that the Holy Spirit provided. By contrast, during hard times he had experienced "a sense of fire" and been "healed". He concluded, in keeping with Ephesians 3:18, that "God's love is long, wide and deep". "Sometimes," he said, "it brings me to tears".

There are several possible physical manifestations of the Spirit. The biblical disciples experienced a "gale that was not a real gale, but it resembled one" and "something… that resembled fire". Some people will "shake like a leaf in the wind", "find themselves breathing deeply as if almost physically breathing in the Spirit", or a heat, or burning on a part or all of their bodies. Others will experience the Spirit on a purely emotional level as "an overwhelming experience of the love of God".[10] But the best illustration of the power of the Holy Spirit was left until last: speaking in tongues.

Malc and I had seen this phenomenon before. As students we once attended a question and answer session called "Grill a Christian". The debate spilled over into the bar afterwards, culminating in an invitation for us to attend a Christian roast dinner to discuss our questions further. When we arrived we were warmly greeted with a "Hi guys!" by a thoroughly nice Christian student with stuffing all over his hands. During dinner he announced that he could speak in tongues, in what he claimed had been identified as an ancient Sumerian dialect. To our astonishment, when challenged he called down the Spirit and gave a spontaneous demonstration. Alas, it just sounded like a rhythmic mumbling, lasting about 30 seconds, which I felt anyone could have made up.[11]

Speaking in tongues is an odd phenomenon for most people, and yet it is a significant aspect of Gumbel's brand of Christianity (he devotes a six pages to it in *Questions of Life*). His insistence on its importance is a controversial point for some churches. For him, tongues are "a form of prayer that transcends the limitation of human language".[12] Mike described how speaking in tongues "builds up" people and "transcends the language barrier" (whatever barrier it transcends it certainly erects a whole new one given that nobody has identified any syntactic structure or semantic content). It was emphasized that there are perfectly good Christians who do not speak in tongues – the Holy Spirit "will not force you" because "he's a gentle man". It is not, we were told, even the "most important gift". Nonetheless, tongues are "a sign for the unbelievers", and they facilitate praise, worship and prayer.

The technical term is glossolalia. The practice re-emerged in the modern era with the birth of the Pentecostal movement in the early part of the 20th century. The appearance of Christian groups speaking in tongues aroused academic interest, and the phenomenon has been studied sporadically ever since. Initially, glossolalia was explained as a result of psychopathology[13] or of altered states of consciousness ("trance" theories). However, glossolalia is rare in psychiatric disorders[14] and can occur in the absence of indicators of altered states,[15] so these viewpoints have now been discounted. The current evidence is strongly in favour of glossolalia simply as a socially learned behaviour that can be acquired by anyone.

In a revealing study, one group of researchers easily taught people glossolalia[16] over a short space of time. A group of university students were first played a 60 second tape of real glossolalia and then attempted to speak in tongues themselves for 30 seconds to gain a baseline measure. Half the students were then provided with two glossolalia training sessions, lasting approximately 30 minutes each, in which they were shown video and audio recordings of real glossolalia and then practised speaking it themselves. While they were practising, the experimenters provided them with encouragement and feedback intended to mimic that given by novice glossolalics in a church setting. The other students acted as controls and were given no training. The fluency of all the students was then assessed by two experienced listeners of glossolalia, one of whom practised it in a religious setting. Those students who received the training were judged far more fluent in tongues compared with those that did not receive training. In fact, after just one hour of training 70% of the students were judged fluent and the rest were at least "moderately proficient". Even more interesting was that, even after only being exposed to the 60 seconds of glossolalia in the baseline measure, 21.6% of the control students were judged fluent glossolalics in the test session.

Mike told us that, in order to receive the gift of tongues, we would need to ask the Lord, to co-operate, to believe, and to persevere. Like any other language, Gumbel says in his book, it takes practice. Hardly: after an hour anybody should have the hang of it, and some might even pick it up after only a minute or two.

Neither is it hard to see the motivation behind becoming a tongues speaker, whether the individuals are aware of it or not. Despite stating that it is not essential, the Alpha course actively encourages and rewards those who practise it. When an attendee starts speaking in tongues it is seen as a milestone on the road to full Christianity. Such an obvious outward sign of sanctification can ease the individual's acceptance by their new peers, and acts to separate their shiny new Christian identity from their past. As one researcher put it "… glossolalia… reinforces a sense of belonging and cohesiveness, and provides recognition from significant others" – in this case other Alpha Christians. Thus there is a palpable social pressure on the attendees for something to happen to them, and certainly for them to at least try speaking in tongues.[17] After they try it many of them will find it remarkably easy to learn.

Given the illogical arguments that many Alpha Christians were willing to accept, it doesn't take a great stretch of imagination to see that they could then convince themselves they really were speaking in tongues and not just murmuring nonsense. If this was coupled with some powerful subjective experience (see the next chapter) it is even easier to see how they could convince themselves.

Mike told us to pray for each other as the band started up again. "There's no pressure," he said, "no obligation, but if you would like to become Christian…" I didn't feel there was no pressure. "Turn to someone you are friends with," he went on soothingly. And so the intense musical worship began again as Mike raised his arms to heaven and let his head fall back. Some members of the congregation sang along to the music while others paired off in corners and hugged. Some were crying. I looked around for tongues, but it was hard to be sure what was being said amid the hubbub. In the background was another sparsely-scored hymn:

Jesus be the centre
Be my source be my light Jesus
Jesus be the centre
Be my song Jesus

Be the fire in my heart
Be the wind in my sails
Be the reason that I live

Jesus Jesus
Jesus be my vision
Be my help
Be my guide Jesus

After twenty minutes of sleepy boredom we crept out, unsure if the session had finished or not. For us, the Holy Spirit had been a no-show.

Notes

1.   God 'fills in' for dentists, BBC website, April 21, 1999. Other manifestations

have included hysterical laughter, physical spasms, crying, and writhing across the stage like a snake.

2. Exodus 31:3-4 "...and I have filled him with the Spirit of God, with skill, ability and knowledge in all kinds of crafts – to make artistic designs for work in gold, silver and bronze..."

3. Judges 6:34: "Then the Spirit of the Lord came upon Gideon, and he blew a trumpet, summoning the Abiezrites to follow him." Sadly this intervention was not altogether successful. Gideon later refused to be king and fathered a child by a concubine. Worse, he constructed a gold idol from his opponents' earrings that incited ungodliness among the Israelites.

4. See Acts 2.

5. Gumbel cites several examples of the Holy Spirit in the Old Testament, but the Hebrew translates as "breath" or "wind", and in one passage to which he alludes the entity is described as the "Angel of the Lord".

6. Hitchens, C. (1995). *The Missionary Position*, Verso Books. The divine light turned out to be a result of a new type of photographic film.

7. Acts 1:8: "But you will receive power when the Holy Spirit comes on you; and you will be my witnesses in Jerusalem, and in all Judea and Samaria, and to the ends of the earth."

8. Acts 8 and 9.

9. Acts 19:1-7.

10. *Questions of Life*, p.146.

11. Here one might ponder Paul's comments in 1 Corinthians 14:6-9: "...if I come to you and speak in tongues, what good will I be to you, unless I bring revelation, prophecy or word of instruction?... Unless you speak intelligible words with your tongue, how will anyone know what you are saying?"

12. *Questions of Life*, p.149. Glossolalia is often conducted in pairs. As the glossolaliac does not know what they are saying, another Christian acts as an "interpreter", using the power of the Holy Spirit to tell everyone what they are saying. Presumably the "Sumerian dialect" in our anecdote was identified by the interpreter.

13. Cutten, G.B. (1927). *Speaking in Tongues*. Yale University Press, New Haven.

14. Richardson, J.T. (1973). Psychological Interpretations of Glossolalia: A Reexamination of Research. *Journal for the Scientific Study of Religion*, 12 (2), 199-207.

15. Spanos, N.P., & Hewitt, E.C. (1979). Glossolalia: A Test of the "Trance" and Psychopathology Hypotheses. *Journal of Abnormal Psychology*, 88 (4), 427-434.

16. Spanos, N.P., Cross, W.P., Lepage, M., & Coristine, M. (1986). Glossolalia as Learned Behaviour: An Experimental Demonstration. *Journal of Abnormal Psychology*, 95 (1), 21-23.

17. Gumbel himself first spoke in tongues while praying alone at home and suggests this as method of introducing oneself to it.

CHAPTER 9

Worshipping Prince

Our Holy Spirit weekend was an anticlimax. The joy of the Holy Spirit had not infused us. Instead the main feeling was one of uneasiness. I later found that this view was shared by other members of our group. Although several people had produced tears and emotional outbursts, I had not definitely seen anyone speaking in tongues. This was disappointing given reports of much wilder weekends, with people "slain in the spirit", uncontrollable swooning, imitations of animals and other bizarre phenomena. In spite of our own unremarkable experience it is still necessary to consider the phenomenon in order to understand the Alpha message.

By now it was clear that personal subjective experiences of God are crucial to the faith of many Alpha Christians. Over the course of our discussions, Bill and others in our group had described events where they had felt the presence of God or experienced visions. If the intellectual arguments for Christianity had so far failed to convert an attendee, a direct feeling of God might just tip the balance, allowing the individual to make the all important "leap of faith". Bill had talked repeatedly of his initial difficulty in understanding Christianity from an intellectual perspective, before visionary dreams finally had him convinced.[1] Sandy had been persuaded when the Holy Spirit had stopped cats purring after a relative died. Clearly the Holy Spirit weekend is intended to provide attendees with their own personal mystical experience in the same vein. In the discussion groups we had been encouraged to talk about emotional subjects; there was the simplistic, repetitive music; and all the hype had produced a strong expectation that something was *meant* to happen.

The history of Christianity is replete with reports of these mystical experiences. A typical example is that of Sister Margareta Ebner, a German nun, who spent several days in silent and constant prayer. She wrote in her diary that one night she had felt the presence of God:

"a great fear came upon me and there in the fear I was surrounded by a grace beyond measure... I felt myself grasped by an inner divine power of God... An immeasurable sweetness was given to me, so that I felt as if my soul was separated from my body. And the sweetest of all names, the name of Jesus Christ, was given to me then with such great fervor of his love..."[2]

Other individuals claiming mystical experiences usually report similar sensations. These "symptoms" are summarized by one author as including "feeling the presence of a personified force which intones a 'higher' power'" (e.g. Jesus), "feeling detached, egoless, at one with the cosmos" (sometimes referred to as a unitary experiences), "feelings of 'timelessness' and 'spacelessness'" and "sensual experiences" including "rapture, ecstasy, elation and bliss".[3]

All this raises the obvious question: are these experiences in any way real? Here we might borrow one of Gumbel's arguments. We could suggest, as he does when discussing Jesus's supposed avowal of his divinity, that people making such claims must be either "mad, bad or telling the truth".[4] No doubt many people alleging mystical experiences are "bad" – they are lying for less than selfless reasons. Stories of religious leaders cheating people out of money for their own benefit are hardly unusual, but what of the followers themselves? Surely they are not all are lying about their experiences, which brings us to the common suggestion that they are simply mad. Many people who consider themselves rationally minded would describe the people involved as ignorant, superstitious, delusional, or perhaps suffering from some form of brain disorder. Indeed it has been the view of many eminent researchers from Freud to modern psychiatrists that it is a form of mass delusion and detrimental to emotional health.[5][6]

At first glance, they have a point. Mystical experiences are associated with numerous clinical conditions. One study has reported that 30% of psychiatric patients reported an increase in religious beliefs;[7] temporal lobe epileptics often experience powerful religious experiences;[8] and religious delusions (including visions and hearing divine voices) are common in patients with a wide variety of mental health disorders.[9] [10] For example, there is the case of one schizophrenic who, realizing his masturbatory activities were a sin, decided to wholeheartedly adopt the "manual for life" approach to the Bible. At first he considered Matthew 18:8 ("If your hand or your foot causes you sin cut it off and throw it away"), but in the end opted for Matthew 19:12 as he considered it a personal reference to himself: "For some are eunuchs because they were born that way; others were made that way by men; and others have renounced marriage because of the Kingdom of Heaven. The one who can accept this should accept it." In response he "incised his scrotum with a razor blade, severed his testicles, and flushed them down the toilet".[11] Pathological brain process *can* produce mystical experiences, but were all the people we met really suffering from some unfortunate form of brain malfunction? Did Bill have temporal lobe epilepsy? Was Tom psychotic?

This blanket explanation of all mystical experience as a result of madness or brain disorder goes too far. It is not convincing when one considers the millions of people claiming them without any other apparent mental problems. Our devoutly religious Alpha organizers appeared, on the surface, to be well functioning individuals. One might also point to studies reporting that, despite possible initial impressions, members of the Charismatic clergy actually come out more stable than the general population when they fill in personality questionnaires.[12] There is also the fact that psychiatric patients reporting mystical experience usually do so in a negative fashion,[13] whereas Bill and the other attendees relished and rejoiced in their experiences.

So these experiences are in some way more "real" than the delusions of the mentally ill, but this is not to suggest there is an absence of scientific explanations – just that they are likely to be subtler. There is no definitive research, but in Appendix D we point to one theory in the psychological literature: that ritualistic settings with the right attributes – notably a repetitive, rhythmic element – have the ability to create mental states conducive to the feelings reported by participants in Alpha Holy Spirit Weekends. This ability depends on the context, but is by no means confined to Evangelical Christian sessions, or even religious settings at all.

This leads us to the most obvious objection to mystical experiences as a justification for Christian belief: people of all religious inclinations report remarkably similar spiritual experiences. Since the dawn of recorded history we have written descriptions of people in all time periods and across all cultures reporting similar experiences. As Matthew Alper puts it "whether it be the born-again experience of the Pentecostal Christian [such as an Alpha Christian], Hindu Samadhi, Sufi fana, or Zen satori, every world culture has described an experience by which individuals claim to feel as if they have been touched by some 'higher' truth or power, an experience almost always identified as spiritual, mystical, religious, or transcendental in nature".[14] These experiences are described in the same terms as mentioned earlier.

There is modern experimental data as well. For instance, brain scans of Tibetan meditators show decreases in activity of a part of the brain termed the orientation association area.[15] This occurs at the peak of meditation when participants report that "it feels like I am part of everyone and everything in existence". Brain scans of Christian nuns at prayer show similar results.[16] During intensely religious experiences the nuns showed the same pattern of reduced activity in the orientation association area. They described the experience as sensing the presence of God and a "mingling of themselves with Him". Both the meditators and the nuns were having neurological experiences that were uncannily similar, and both described a sense of their self merging with something else.

Fundamentally, the types of sensations and feelings described by Christians – feelings of awe, oneness with others, etc. – in no way inform us about Christianity unless we choose to interpret them in this way. Taken alone they say nothing specific about Christianity[17] and thus provide no argument for adopting the doctrines of the Bible. (On top of this, the Bible is actually unclear on what sort of mystical experiences one is likely to have, leading to widely differing interpretations even within Evangelical Protestantism.)

They don't even necessarily point in a religious direction. Consider the following descriptions of transcendent experiences:

1. "….and last an internal peace that words cannot describe"
2. "It made me ecstatic, inconceivably exhilarated, everything concentrated in a single now"

3. "my head is gone, my body too and yet I am here…the whole room, the whole universe is present here in perfect harmony…I seem to be experiencing directly and have no words to express this state of bliss, harmony…"

4. "you are filled with the wonderful feeling that everything is all right"

5. "It feels like I am a part of everyone and everything in existence"

6. "I was no longer in my previous….state but was…lcd to find a peace…and was content with everything".

One is the description of a meditator at the peak of his meditative experience, one of a nun praying. The other four are from individuals' descriptions of their most intense responses listening to and playing music (Bach, Mozart and the pop star Prince).[18] Distinguishing them is not easy.[19] That is because the meditation, prayer and music are likely triggering very similar neurological processes. If the capacity to produce mystical experiences is one's sole guide to spiritual truth – and it does appear to be for some Christians – then one might as well worship Prince.

In summary, it is a mistake to use this type of experience as a basis for belief in the Bible, because they usually act as a mirror to one's background, not a guide to transcendental truth. Faced with a spiritual experience, Christians will almost inevitably reach for an interpretation in terms of the Christian god. Followers of other religions will look elsewhere. On the pacific island of Tanna, followers of the Jon Frum cult see "Jon". Jon is a messianic figure whom prophets report seeing at night, often wearing a wide-brimmed hat to (conveniently) hide his face. He is supposed to return one day and usher in a time when unlimited "cargo" will arrive from the United States and people will have everything they want. He has also periodically appeared in order to provoke resistance against the British colonial authorities and Christian missionaries.[20] The myth was formed out of bafflement with Second World War technology, and yet it persists today as an example of how people interpret the apparently inexplicable in terms of what they know.

When Sandy's relative died and the cats stopped purring she sought

94

an explanation and a vicar supplied one in terms of Christian dogma. After that she was convinced that she had sensed the Christian god, not Jon Frum or Allah. The same was true of Graham's martial arts experience. Then there was Bill. As we later heard, he had once "sensed a cold presence" in a man while carrying out a Christian survey in the street. His description of this experience was "it was just something – it's difficult to describe – it was a feeling I had. I don't say this lightly, but I've never felt this before. But when I spoke to him I just felt a chill across my soul". Bill had decided that he had sensed a demon and had developed an entire Bible-inspired back story on the subject of demons. But why? His "feeling" itself said nothing about the Bible, so why attribute it to a demon and use it to bolster his faith in Christianity? He, Sandy, and Graham used the Bible to explain their experience, and they had used their experience to justify belief in the Bible's truth – a circular argument, like so much of Alpha.

Notes

1. See Chapter 13 for Bill's demonic encounters.
2. Cited in Newberg, A., D'Aquili, E. & Rause, V. (2001). *Why God Won't Go Away.* Ballantine Books, New York.
3. These quotes were obtained from Alper, M. (2006). *The "God" Part of the Brain.* Sourcebooks Inc, Naperville, Illinois. In his book Alper provides far more detail on descriptions of mystical experiences and other "symptoms" include a sense of "sacredness", "awareness of a higher power or ultimate reality", and a "sense that one cannot adequately describe the richness of their experience".
4. We are quoting Tom, but Gumbel says the same in a more long-winded manner on p.32 of *Questions of Life.* In any case, the argument is borrowed from C.S.Lewis – see chapter 2.
5. Freud, S. Civilization, Society and Religion: Group Psychology, *Civilization and its discontents and other works.* (1991). The Penguin Freud Library Vol 12. Penguin books
6. Ellis A. Do some religious beliefs help create emotional disturbance? *Psychotherapy in Private Practice* (1986); 4:101-6
7. Kirov, G., Kemp, R., Kirov, K., & David, A. (1998). Religious faith after psychotic illness. *Psychopathology,* 31, 234-245.
8. The most famous case being Fyodor Dostoevsky. See Appendix D for more information.
9. Brewerton, T.D., (1994). Hyperreligiosity in psychotic disorders. *Journal of Nervous and Mental Disease* 182, 302-304.

10. Siddle R., Haddock, G., Tarrier, N., & Faragher, B.E. (2002) Religious delusions in patients admitted to hospital with schizophrenia, *Social Psychiatry and Psychiatric Epidemiology* 37(3), 130-138.

11. Waugh, A. (1986). Autocastration and Biblical delusions in schizophrenia. *British Journal of Psychiatry,* 149, 656-659. It should be noted that Origen, a respected church father, also castrated himself on the basis of the same bible passage.

12. For examples see: Francis, L.J., & Thomas, T.H. (1997). Are charismatic ministers less stable? A study among male Anglican clergy. *Review of Religious Research,* 39 (1), 61-69; Musson, D.J. (1998). The personality profile of male Anglican clergy in England. *Personality and Individual Differences,* 25 (4), 698-698.

13. Some have gouged out their own "sinful eyes" or attacked others, such as the Texan mother who drowned her five children in order to save their souls from Satan. See Appendix D for more detail.

14. For a good summary see Alper, M. (2006). *The "God" Part of the Brain,* Sourcebooks Inc, Naperville, Illinois.

15. Newberg A., Alavi A. Baime, M. Pourdehnad, M. Santanna & J. D'Aquili E. (2001). The measurement of regional cerebral blood flow during the complex cognitive task of meditation: A preliminary SPECT study. *Psychiatry Research: Neuroimaging,* 106 (2), 113-122.

16. Newberg, A., Pourdehnad, M., Alavi, A. & D'Aquili, E. (2003). Cerebral blood flow during meditative prayer: preliminary findings and methodological issues. *Perceptual and Motor Skills,* 97 (2), 625-63.

17. We might here make an exception if an Angel or God actually spoke to an individual, but in those cases we have a much stronger case for the "mad" or "bad" hypotheses.

18. These quotes are taken from Gabrielson (2001) and two of Newberg et al's (2001) studies.

19. 1-4 are music related quotes, 5 is the meditator and 6 is the nun.

20. The Jon Frum cult is one of several Pacific Island religions that have been termed "Cargo Cults".

CHAPTER 10

What if this man really is Jesus and I'm giving him injections?

The Spirit didn't lead many to Alpha for the next session – the congregation was reduced to a rump of the extremely committed. But we found Clive, "cynical" Pete's brother-in-law, in chatty mood. He enthused about his home study "cell" group. They were studying John's Gospel to coincide with Mike's Sunday sermons. He was keen to stress that this home study was a no-pressure gathering of chums who just got together and talked about what it all meant, but it seemed safe to assume these freewheeling chats would be well within the boundaries of scepticism-free Evangelical Christianity.

Cell groups are designed to subdivide and multiply, hence the name. Because the strictures of traditional church worship were seen as jarring to those from non-Christian backgrounds, the cell group was devised to spread Christianity organically, without confronting potential converts with the trappings of organized services. The Alpha training material[1] makes clear the need to suck in unbelieving friends and eventually expand each group until it can subdivide and start again, amoeba-like. As with Alpha, unbelievers are eased towards fundamentalism via unthreatening chitchat after recruitment via normal social channels. Then they can pass on the message to others. Drift of members is discouraged via "discipling" and personal relationships.

If this sounds like a disease, then it's worth pointing out that Christians aren't necessarily against being tagged agents of infection. An entire franchise is based on this angle. Available in the HTB bookshop is *Becoming a Contagious Christian*,[2] which advises how to "develop a contagious Christian character" and "learn to direct conversations to matters of faith". One chapter is titled "Strategic Opportunities in Relationships". The faith contagion brand is further promoted in various DVDs, audio tapes, manuals and study guides. Other authors have produced the management-speak version, *The Three Habits of Highly Contagious Christians*,[3] and the thrilling *Outbreak: Creating a Contagious Youth Ministry Through Viral Evangelism*,[4] not to mention *Contagious Witness*, *Contagious Joy* and *Contagious Generosity*.[5]

As I evaded Clive's bid to disciple me, we were joined by Pete, Belinda and Nadine. Pete was poking morosely at his bread rolls (he'd missed the meal). Everybody agreed the Holy Spirit Weekend had been draining. Rather than pumped full of spiritual energy, people in our group seemed to have left exhausted. None of them had burst into tears or prayed for one another, but they'd seen many others do it. Belinda leaned forward and confided that the whole band had been in tears as helpers massaged their shoulders: "It was spooky!" Nadine was no more impressed, saying it had been "uncomfortable". We all agreed that the morning had been OK, but the final talk had been too much. Nobody seemed happy with the idea of speaking in tongues.

But this hadn't entirely put Pete off Charismatic Christianity, because that same evening he'd joined his brother-in-law at a service called "Hillsong" in Leatherhead: "The only way I can think of putting it is, you know there's sport and extreme sport, right? Well this was extreme worship!" It had involved a Christian rock band and, most amazing of all, mass singing in tongues. I immediately resolved to get to this church, but Pete seemed in two minds about the experience. "I'm normally quite a reserved person," he said in clear contravention of the facts, "and all these people had their hands in the air, but I just stood there stiff." He hadn't liked the strenuous tin-rattling either, with multiple exhortations, and donations envelopes on every seat, but the music was "amazing". He happily suggested that we go there on a sort of group field trip.

All through this conversation there had been a desire to chatter rising up inside Belinda. When a lull arrived, she burst forward with a long tale of her background in "bandit country" near the Northern Irish border, and how her sister had secured a £40,000 grant to renovate a £5,000 house, and was now a minor property magnate with fifteen houses. Any responses offered were discarded, or used as cues for a further tumult of detail. Then we were onto her international travels – working cleaning ships in Denmark ("not a beautiful country, but the people are lovely"), pondering a life on a Kibbutz, teaching some Scandinavians to speak with a "broad Irish accent" ("it was very funny"), and finally meeting her English ex-husband: "It's ever so funny, because now I live here and he's in Ireland!" I didn't get the impression she very much cared whom she told these stories, just as long as she could keep telling them. The main benefit of Alpha for her seemed to be a new audience. It was a relief to sidle off to the talk, where we took seats next to Bill.

Tom began with a joke of ancient vintage. Mike, we were told, had been marooned on his roof by a flooded river. Three potential rescuers had come by on rafts, boats and helicopters – each described in loving detail – but he had refused their help, saying that God would surely save a Christian minister personally. When he had drowned (the thought of this provoked a few chortles) and gone to heaven he reproached God, who told him that he had indeed tried to help: "I sent a raft, a boat and a helicopter!"

As the congregation wiped away their tears, Mike stepped up to tell us about how God[6] promised in Psalms 32:8 to help out with life's big decisions:

"I will instruct you and teach you in the way you should go; I will counsel you and watch over you."

Naturally, we are not to fear this guidance because God has a "good plan" for us, at least if we believe Jeremiah 29:11 ("My favourite verse!" whispered Bill) and Romans 12:2.[7]

I sat there wondering how uniformly good God's plans are for us. For instance, why did God's "good plan" include electrocuting his own pastor, Reverend Kyle Lake? During a 2005 service in Waco, Texas, Lake grabbed a microphone while standing waist deep in baptismal water, and was immediately fried in front of 800 people. He left behind a wife and three young children. One might have expected them to seek answers in the book he wrote the previous year, *Understanding*

God's Will; actually they sued the electrical contractor. God presumably willed that.

Christians, at least those who haven't seen a family member cut down while delivering God's message, usually see such incidents as God's will in some complex, counter-intuitive sense that doesn't disprove his goodness. Sudden windfalls or miraculous healings will be seen in quite another, far more straightforward light. So it proved at Alpha.

When interpreting God's apparently twisted sense of humour, Mike was clear that "knowing God's heart actually helps". The problem is that "if we're not sure what his voice sounds like we're not sure what to do". It is imperative that we learn to identify his guiding voice, because Isaiah[8] indicates that every major decision should follow a consultation with God. There is no need to question the goodness of God's plan because he has by definition the best plan for our lives. Our attitude must thus be one of humility as we seek to know his will. (Humility seems appropriate, given God's will as specified elsewhere in Isaiah, where he insists on three years' nudity for his prophet, "as a sign and portent against Egypt and Ethiopia". This divinely mandated mooning is cited as a model for the king of Assyria, whom God says must finish the job by parading Egyptians and Ethiopians "with buttocks bared".[9])

So how do we identify what God's "voice sounds like"? Mike revealed five ways we can discover his guidance, all conveniently abbreviated with the letters CS – commanding scripture, controlling spirit, common sense, counsel of saints, and circumstantial signs.

According to Gumbel, "God's general will for all people in all in places in all circumstances is revealed" in the Bible in the form of "Commanding Scripture".[10] On this Gumbel is categorical: "[God] has told us what he thinks about a whole range of issues. From the Bible we know that certain things are wrong." In the case of adultery, for instance, "God has already made his will clear. He has said, 'You shall not commit adultery' (Exodus 20:14).[11] We can be quite sure that God will not guide us to commit adultery".[12]

Yet again this brings us back to the less palatable rulings of the Bible.[13] On the subject of marital guidance, the Bible is clear that adultery is wrong, but it also instructs: "Wives, submit to your husbands as to the Lord."[14] Presumably we can be "quite sure that God will not guide us" to think wives should *not* be subject to their husbands. The same must apply to Jesus's strictures on divorce, now ignored by almost all Protestants. But it was a safe bet that if I raised these examples of Commanding Scripture in the discussion group there would be objections. In short, God's "particular will" is rather less well defined than Gumbel claims. Nevertheless, we were assured that "anything which is contradictory to his word is against his will".

Contradictions are especially relevant when considering the next conduit for divine instruction: "Controlling Spirit". When employing this method God instils thoughts, desires and feelings in a person. But according to Mike they need to be tested against various criteria, including whether they are "loving", whether they are "strengthening, encouraging and comforting", and whether they bring "the peace of God".

Mike gave his ordination as an example of God's hand being on the tiller of his life. He'd had the overwhelming desire to become a vicar, and his Christian friends had asked him, "Have you considered ordination?" He was sure God wanted him to pursue this path. Yet on his first attempt he had failed. This was only an example of poor timing, however, because in fact God had wanted him to become a vicar a little later, as he had found when he tried for the second time and succeeded. What happens is God's will; whatever doesn't happen isn't. This provides a handy retrospective justification for everything, but how useful is it in determining one's future actions? Somehow the devout must distinguish feelings and desires inspired by God from those caused by Satan or, say indigestion.

More fortunate Christians would be guided in more overt ways, and Mike provided plenty of examples of visions, dreams, angels and voices in the Bible, but he gave few contemporary examples. God seems to have veered from this more obvious sort of communiqué since his glory days in the Bible, just as he has stopped parting seas and handing down stone tablets.

It was important to remember that these signs from the Spirit were not given "to avoid the strain of thinking". In order to interpret them properly we would need "Common Sense". To illustrate the problem, Mike mentioned a woman who prayed for guidance before putting on each item of clothing in the morning, often going out wearing a single stocking as a consequence. There was also the person who made decisions by opening the Bible at random pages and following what was said on that page – and hit the Judas suicide story. The audience tittered, but of course these were the most harmless of God's misguided servants. History is littered with self-described Christians impelled by faith to mass murder, and they have always been able to point to Yahweh's own genocidal campaigns as justification.

Besides, the Bible is full of strange stories in which God's followers ignored common sense at his specific request. The most obvious example, which also shows the difficulties with the "love" test, is that of Abraham and his only son Isaac. In Genesis 22 God instructed Abraham, who had waited an unnaturally long time to have a son, to convert that son into a burnt offering. Failing to apply common sense or any recognizable concept of love, he immediately set off to kill his son. God relented, but his point was clear: blind obedience explicitly was needed in his followers. Conclusions based on "love" are clearly not always a good indicator of his will, which had been demonstrated repeatedly to be incomprehensible, if not sadistic. Alongside this, of course, common sense dictates that we not believe in miracles like walking on water, feeding thousands with a few loaves of bread, or the resurrection, without exceptionally strong evidence, which isn't available. These sorts of problem were not acknowledged in the talk. Rather, "common sense" functioned as an escape hatch for when the Bible or allegedly spiritual urges offended normality.

The most verbally tenuous "CS" was the "Counsel of Saints", which boiled down to asking one's friends for advice, the only twist being that "the best advisors are usually godly Christian people". Gumbel's only example was of a wise old friend he turned to from time to time who offered unspecified pointers.

Finally, Christians should take into account "Circumstantial Signs". The tale was recounted of Michael Bourdeaux, later an adviser to Margaret Thatcher, visiting Russia. While there in 1964 he had coincidentally met two women who had written to him six months earlier. Being a Christian he'd taken it as a sign from God. (If he hadn't been a Christian he'd presumably have taken it to be or astrological fate, or whatever.) Christians should watch for this sort of hint, keeping in mind that God confusingly both opens (1 Corinthians 16:9) and closes (Acts 16:7) doors. Mike related this back to his ordination troubles. As ever, God's ambiguous signalling methods seem calculated to leave even the devout unsure, because first time around he had been sure he was doing God's will, yet he hadn't been, because God wanted him to fail. He didn't doubt, however, that "God works in all things for the good of those who love him". The conclusion wouldn't have been complete without the appropriate cliché: "Sometimes God works in very, very mysterious ways."

Before Bill could begin the discussion group we were interrupted by angry bearded Martin, who peremptorily told us he wasn't joining the group, fiddled with a fuse on the wall, and left. I was disappointed we wouldn't have his hard-line views represented in the discussion. We were also missing Sandy, her husband and Wilma.

There was a prolonged silence, as nobody seemed to have any strong views on God's guidance. "Can we talk about the weekend first?" asked Malc. "We were talking about it earlier and we are very intrigued by the idea of speaking in tongues. Can you tell us exactly what it is and how it works? Do people speak in other human languages? Or is it something else?" The others murmured agreement, saying they'd found it hard to understand.

Bill seemed slightly uncomfortable talking about this. "It can seem a little bizarre, but I see it as a kind of heavenly language," he said, after hesitating. "It's a way of expressing yourself when words aren't enough. It's only one of the gifts of the Holy Spirit, and not everybody does it." Some people only gained it, he told us, "for a season". Still others, he warned, were not using it "for the glory of God" but instead on their own account. It wasn't obvious how gabbling incomprehensibly benefited them, or why the Holy Spirit continued to infuse them with the ability.

Pete wasn't satisfied: "It sounds like a light sabre! What's the point of it?" Then he launched again into his description of the Hillsong experience: "The only way I can put it – I was saying to them – is, there's sport and there's extreme sport, right? Well this was extreme worship!" He told Bill about being too reserved to fully join in. He'd found it strange, the number of tongues-speakers there.

"Exactly," said Bill, "and it's my firm belief…" – he paused, looked down, and began again, earnestly gesturing with a hand held out in front of him – "that some people only use the gift of tongues for personal glory, or because they feel they have to do it to be a Christian. So not everybody in the crowd could have been talking in tongues." He reiterated what Mike had said at the weekend about the dangers of misusing tongues.

Pete then admitted he'd found the weekend session a letdown. "To be frank," he said, "I was expecting something to happen and when it didn't I was disappointed." He thought that the people at Hillsong might have been speaking in tongues partly because they badly wanted to, not because God was moving them.

Belinda weighed in with her views on spiritual manifestations. "When I was little we had paintings like that," she began, pointing at an innocuous oil painting on the wall of the vestry, "and I used to be very scared. We had all these stories about local spirits, and I really didn't want them or an angel to come to me. I used to lie there hoping they wouldn't come!"

Bill nodded sympathetically. "So it's all tangled up with local mythology?" he asked. Belinda nodded, but showed no interest in expanding on that aspect.

"Back to this week's talk, have any of you experienced God's guidance?" said Bill.

"Now, I don't want this to turn into an AA meeting," Pete began, "but eight months ago I was in a really bad place. I was feeling really depressed. But I've had a complete change. If you guys had seen me six months ago you'd have said I was a different person – not outgoing at all!" He didn't specify how God had been involved in this transformation, but it was enough to secure a nod from Bill as we considered it.

Belinda had another anecdote ready: "I do feel guidance sometimes" was one of her few concessions to relevance. "I was looking for my driving licence, because I'd got three points for speeding, and I had to send it off, but I couldn't find it, and I was looking everywhere – you know, in completely ridiculous places", she rolled her eyes and waved her hand dismissively, "and in the same places over and over again – and I couldn't find it. I sent this licence off – the paper bit – but they sent it back because I hadn't sent the photo bit, and all this took weeks, and I was worried, you know, they would fine me. And I called the police people."

There intervened a discussion with Nadine and Bill about why they needed the photo bit – was it to put information on the magnetic strip? Nobody was sure.

"Anyway, I was looking for it everywhere, and then I said a prayer to Saint Andrew – you know, we [Catholics] pray to Saint Andrew when we lose things – and I looked in the car, and in the car was a cardigan, and it was just hanging out of it. So I do think I get some guidance. Because, you know, I was so worried I'd be fined, and I'd looked everywhere. So I think some higher being was looking after me."

We listened in glazed silence until she ran out of details to add, whereupon Bill jumped in before she could gather steam again. His problem had been far more serious than a mislaid driving licence. "Earlier this year, in January, I was going through a divorce that I didn't want," he began in a serious tone. "And for ten days – I know the date exactly – I felt a disconnection from God. I was praying and I wasn't feeling anything there. After ten days I had this dream where I was standing under a boulder, and the boulder disappeared, and after that I had a tremendous sense of peace." He was smiling now. "Ever since then, with all the rejection and so on I've been able to call on that feeling of peace whenever I've wanted."

This had allowed Belinda time for another rummage in her mental attic. "I had an aunt… she was a wicked woman who didn't talk to anyone but prayed all day – you know. And she lived in a small house – a really small house, I mean it had just two rooms, you know – and it was in a field with no roads to it. Anyway, one day a nun came by and gave her a crucifix with a relic of Saint Martin in it. And she went up to the nunnery and they'd never heard of the nun! After that she was nice to everybody, and people started coming to touch the cross and, you know, be healed. In the end she had to put up a mobile home on the land the nun left her!"

As soon as she reached the denouement, she was off again about her job as a psychiatric nurse. "And I do wonder, you know. All these people who say they're Jesus – we have people coming in who say they're

Jesus or whatever. I mean, all these people claiming they're Jesus, and I wonder, 'What if they are?' What if this man really is Jesus and I'm giving him injections?"

The room erupted in laughter. Belinda seemed surprised and finally faltered, giving Malc the chance to ask, "I was wondering, with these signs and things, can you attribute it to the Christian God guiding you – why not something else?"

"But it's often hard to convince scientists isn't it?" asked Nadine, apparently seeing a connection.

Bill wasn't going to agree with that: "Actually, what we're finding now more and more – at least what seems to me to be coming out – is that the more we look into these things, the more evidence there is that there's a higher power driving things." This seemed an extraordinary statement to make. To what was he referring? Young earth Creationism? Stephen Hawking's slightly extravagant rhetoric in *A Brief History of Time* about knowing "the mind of God"? The history of science was clearly one of retrieving phenomena from religion's domain, so what had changed?

Pete was convinced. "There's actually a guy doing – what is it? – particle physics doing the course. What's his name?"

"Gordon."

"Gordon – that's it."

Nadine nodded. It was settled: even science loved Christianity.

I felt I had to ask about God's less obviously beneficial interventions: "I was wondering, about this idea that God has a good plan for us... There was a story in the news about a pastor in America doing a baptism who was electrocuted. I just don't know how we interpret God's will there."

"What happened?" asked Pete.

"He asked for a microphone and just got electrocuted, is how I understand it."

"Completely frazzled," nodded Bill sadly.

Pete suggested it was a circumstantial sign, although of what he didn't say. Malc said it pointed to the need for Mike's "Common Sense", which was fair enough, but it didn't let God off the hook for allowing his representative to die so pointlessly. It wasn't as if this was the only example of God's peculiar inclinations. I mentioned the case of God inciting David to conduct a census for which he punished not David, but 70,000 other people, with death (2 Samuel 24), but Bill's only answer was to dispute that God was responsible for causing David to perform the census.[15]

The group didn't have any fundamental questioning of premises. There was a set of assumptions – a loving God, biblical truth, etc. – that might lead to difficult questions, but those questions would never cause the assumptions to be reconsidered; they were just something interesting to be discussed, resolved if possible, but never taken seriously enough to rock the foundations. How did such a discussion qualify as an exploration of the "meaning of life", as Alpha advertised?

In any case, our time was up. This week everybody seemed to be keen to go to the pub so we moved our investigations there. Once Bill had sat down with us we soon returned to the subject of Mount Sinai. Were the Saudis actually hiding the real one? Bill admitted he had a few reservations as he'd drawn the information from a "semi-popular book", but he'd found it pretty convincing. The Egyptian Mount Sinai, in the Sinai Peninsula, wasn't in a roomy enough location. The Saudi Arabian one, which was in a much more plausible area, had been cordoned off as part of a military base. The significance of all this remained obscure, however.

We moved onto Bill's theological qualifications. Malc asked if he had, in the light of Mike's story, considered becoming a Vicar himself. Bill gave a little laugh and muttered darkly, "Not the way I am now!" As so often with his personal life, his meaning was obscure.

After Pete joined us the conversation eventually arrived at Gordon's journey, via the spiritual aspects of ninjitsu, to Christianity. What did Bill think about these supernatural phenomena? He hedged carefully: "I don't know exactly, but I'd be wary – I think it might not be the Holy Spirit."

"You think it's maybe demonic then?"

"As I say, it's not easy to be sure, but I think it could be, yes."

I looked forward to taking up the subject of demons with Bill next week, where we were to learn how to resist evil. In the meantime he had to go. We agreed to go to Hillsong with Pete next week and headed off. To be fair to Alpha, it doesn't exactly deny the fog of unpleasant biblical rules, misleading feelings, and ambiguous signals that make up

God's guidance. It's just utterly unconvincing when selling them as loving and helpful or, in the case of feelings and coincidences, in any way conclusive.

Notes

1. *How To Run The Alpha Course.*
2. Hybells, B. & Mittelberg, M. (1996). *Becoming A Contagious Christian.* Zondervan Publishing House.
3. Poole G.D. (2003). *The Three Habits Of Highly Contagious Christians: A Discussion Guide For Small Groups.* Zondervan Publishing House.
4. Stier, G. (2006). *Outbreak: Creating a Contagious Youth Ministry Through Viral Evangelism.* Moody Publishers.
5. Women of Faith. (2006). *Contagious Joy.* W Publishing Group. Crandall, R. (1999). *Contagious Witness.* Abingdon Press; Stone, D.L, & Cameron, B.L. (2006). *Contagious Generosity,* Heartspring Publishing.
6. The rest of Psalm 32 is addressed by a sinner to God, not the other way round (e.g. Part of Psalm 32:5 reads "I said, 'I will confess my transgressions to the Lord,' and you forgave the guilt of my sin."), muddying the meaning.
7. Jeremiah 29:12: "Then you will call upon me and come and pray to me, and I will listen to you." Romans 12:2: "Do not conform any longer to the pattern of this world, but be transformed by the renewing of your mind. Then you will be able to test and approve what God's will is – his good, pleasing, perfect will."
8. Isaiah 30:1: "'Woe to the obstinate children', declares the Lord, 'to those who carry out plans that are not mine, forming an alliance, but not by my Spirit, heaping sin upon sin'".
9. Isaiah 20:2-5: "'Take off the sackcloth from your body and the sandals from your feet'. And he did so, going around stripped and barefoot. Then the Lord said, 'just as my servant Isaiah has gone stripped and barefoot for three years, as a sign and portent against Egypt and Cush, so the King of Assyria will lead away stripped and barefoot the Egyptian captives and Cushite exiles, young and old, with buttocks bared – to Egypt's shame.'"
10. *Questions of Life* p.102.
11. Exodus 20:14: "You shall not commit adultery". Gumbel chooses to cite the more saleable Biblical pronouncements on adultery, but not the death sentence imposed for that crime in Leviticus 20:10: "If a man commits adultery with the wife of his neighbour, both the adulterer and the adulteress shall be put to death." This is reiterated in Deuteronomy 22:22, followed by the specific provision that betrothed fake virgins should be stoned at the town gate. Nowhere does Alpha explain why God's frequent resort to the death penalty – e.g. to "purge" rebellious sons (Deuteronomy 21:18-21) – is no longer his will. It's not as if biblically-mandated death is historically unheard of in the Christian era taken as a whole.

12. *Questions of Life*, p.102.
13. See Chapters 4 and 6 on the problem of defining sin and viewing the bible as a "manual for life". See also Appendix C.
14. Ephesians 5:22.
15. Translations disagree over who incited David, but the majority favour God as the culprit, not unreasonably because a pronoun meaning "he" is used at the beginning of the chapter when no other subject has been introduced. Attempts to blame Satan are tenuous, based on reading 1 Chronicles, which was a later book that drew on Samuel. Of course, non-hard-line Christians could admit Biblical fallibility whereas Bill took the only avenue left open to fundamentalists. Whoever did make David commit the infraction, it was not clear why it was even a crime or why 70 000 innocent people had to pay for it while David escaped.

CHAPTER 11

We've come to a gunfight with a knife!

All the occupied tables were full this week, so we sat down alone with our anaemic chilli. While queuing for cakes and coffee we ran into the friendlier Alpha faction of Pete, Clive and his partner Jo. Pete wasn't happy about his journey back from London. "Some pillock pulled the safety cord," he grumbled. "Obviously no one owned up so the guard had to check every carriage."

He brightened when Hillsong came up. "So are we ready for our mutiny this week?" he asked. While he had thoroughly bought into Christianity – he hardly seemed to have much choice given his relations – he also relished playing the rebel. "We should go with t-shirts printed up with 'Unbeliever'!" he joked. We assured him we were still keen to go and agreed between us to raise it in the discussion group.

Soon we were called, against a backing of jazzy music, to sit down for the talk. Of course we couldn't begin without some rib tickling from Mike, who'd dug deep for his retaliation against Tom. Tom had, said a grinning Mike, withdrawn £1,000 from a bank, neatly bound by an elastic band. But what was this? He'd dropped it. Hurrying back for the money he'd been accosted by a man outside the bank.

"Have you lost a thousand pounds in an elastic band?" asked the stranger

"Yes!" said Tom.

"Well I found the elastic band," said his interlocutor, hilariously. Even the regulars didn't seem impressed with this one.

Perhaps they were intent on the solemn topic of the day, "How Can I Resist Evil?" Tom followed the *Questions of Life* script closely, although he seemed embarrassed to be talking about the Devil – for the culprit was this malignant entity. (In the book Nicky Gumbel emphasizes the one letter difference between "evil" and "devil", "good" and "God", as if these linguistic coincidences confined to the English speaking world have any meaning.[1]) We should be in no doubt, Tom told us, that the Devil was a real entity, even if we found the old images of a man with horns silly. He admitted that he'd struggled with this concept, but seemed prepared to affirm his belief in it now. He mysteriously conceded, "I've found it difficult to believe in the Devil, so maybe some of this is addressed to me."

To what extent, I wondered, was this transition determined by expedience? If you were an Anglican minister of moderate inclination, was there a temptation to mould your theological views to the requirements of Alpha, simply because it seemed to stem the flow of people away from your church? The sociological study *Anyone for Alpha* and the guide for running the Alpha Course[2] make clear that the extent to which practitioners are allowed to modify the course is limited. Perhaps a university chaplain like Tom had no choice but to go along with Alpha if he wanted to be relevant.

Whatever the reasons for Tom's changed views, he assured us that the Devil is a "personal spiritual being, active and alive in the world". As might be expected, Tom was referring to the New Testament depiction of the Devil, which was conflated with the rather different Satan of the Old Testament. The clash is most evident when considering the nature of Satan in Job, where he incited God to test Job's commitment to his faith. God then gave Satan licence as a kind of co-conspirator to inflict on Job infamous hardship with the words "everything he has is in your hands, but on the man himself do not lay a finger".[3] This doer of God's work is a very different figure from the source of evil in the New Testament.

Just as God transforms from a capricious, brutal despot to a gentle loving helper as we enter the era of Jesus, so the morally ambiguous Satan – who as far as the accounts go did far less damage than God in the Old Testament[4] – mutates into a vicious figure tempting Jesus and causing much of the world's misery. Inevitably one asks why, if the Hebrew bible actually prefigures the Greek scriptures, Satan should change in such a fundamental way. But naturally we were enjoined to view the Devil in the scarier sense that screams for godly protection.

"Don't be shocked," Tom told us, "when you feel under attack." – for the Devil is cunning and evil and powerful, and commands demons. 1 Peter 5:8 warns that "the devil prowls around like a roaring lion looking for someone to devour". Demons are a problem because "as soon as we start to serve God their interest is aroused".

Why, according to Alpha, should we believe in the Devil? First, there is scripture, which as noted presents wildly differing pictures of this creature. Secondly, "common sense" – so important on isolated occasion in Christian apologetics – apparently dictates the existence of the Fallen One. Partly this was because, as Tom said, "any theology without the Devil has a lot to explain"; that is, the Devil is a useful excuse for earthly suffering. "Common sense" told me that a loving god who was more than a match for the Devil (after Jesus defeated him on the cross we'd apparently been in a two thousand year "mopping up" operation) would not allow such an entity to continue to exist.

Finally, Christians "down the ages" have believed in the Devil. Of course, Christians "down the ages" have believed all sorts of things pertaining to manifestations of evil. For example, there is the *Malleus Maleficarum*,[5] a how-to guide for demon hunters. Written by deranged Inquisitors Heinrich Kramer and Jacob Sprenger, it is a bizarre guide to the Devil, witches, demons and how they should be dealt with. It was embraced by the Catholic Church in its witch-hunts and also used and much admired by Protestants. In the form of a series of questions and answers backed by biblical references it provides a detailed discussion of important topics such as "Whether children can be generated by Incubi and Succubi", "Why is it that Women are chiefly addicted to Evil superstitions?",[6] and the important concern, present in any committed Christian's mind, of "Whether Witches may work some Prestidigatory Illusion so that the Male Organ appears to be entirely removed and separate from the Body".

Amid a stream of eyebrow-raising revelations one learns that "no one does more harm to the Catholic Faith than midwives", how witches deprive men of their "virile members", and how demons seduce men and steal their semen to impregnate other creatures. The latter part of the book outlines how witches should be tried and punished. It is a sex-obsessed and outlandish work, rampant with misogyny. The view it presents of supernatural evil, however, is not fundamentally different from Alpha's. They both suggest that the Devil is an autonomous being, interfering directly in the world and commanding an army of demons. The essential difference is over tactics and presentation, not ideology, as the reference to belief "down the ages" suggests. Taken seriously, the Alpha view of demons would not reach its terminus in feel-good guitar strumming Anglican services; it would instead mandate pitched spiritual battle. Indeed, we saw part of the natural progression among the group leadership as the course went on.

Back in the talk, Tom sternly informed us that The Dark One was "the source of evil regimes" and responsible for "institutional torture, violence" and "mass murders", forgetting that these were acts the Old Testament God repeatedly endorsed and engaged in. Does Satan's responsibility for "terrorist atrocities" extend to God's destruction of Jericho and other cities?[7] Doesn't "sexual and physical abuse of children" cover what Lot proposed for his daughters, and Abraham for Isaac?[8] What of the Inquisition and the bloody carnage of the crusades? Were these instituted by Satan too?

Of Gumbel's charge sheet the only category that can be laid solely at Satan's door is "occult activity and satanic rituals" – that is, activities causing no obvious material harm that are practically by definition related to Satan according to Alpha dogma. In a typically superficial concession towards moderation, there is a brief warning that one's interest in these matters could become too great. But the essential message is that a "war" is being fought against a vicious evil creature who commands an army of demons.

Content that he had demonstrated the existence of Satan, Tom turned to how we could resist his diabolical schemes. Prayer somehow damages the Devil, but alongside launching these directed attacks Christians must totally disassociate themselves from his works. They must "repent and destroy anything associated with the occult", "such as books, charms, videos and magazines".[9] This focus on the dark arts seemed to imply that occult practices actually worked, and were not harmless nonsense, as "common sense" told me they were. Instead, "spiritualism, palm-reading, Ouija boards, 'channelling' [consulting the dead], astrology, horoscopes, witchcraft and occult powers" exist and are demonic in origin.

So what is Satan achieving with his horoscopes and Ouija boards?

According to the Bible he aims to "destroy", blinds people to the "light of the Gospel" – and worst of all – causes doubt. This last was justified by reference to Genesis, which doesn't mention the Devil,[10] and passages in Matthew which talk about the Devil tempting Jesus, but only imply doubt in a loose sense.[11] The Devil induces doubt because, Tom said, "he wants us to agree with him and say, 'Oh no, I can't be a Christian'". It leads catastrophically to "scepticism and cynicism". The usual "balanced" rider was attached, of course. "Don't get me wrong," he hurried on to say, "asking questions is fine", but he was against "scepticism with the desire to knock down everything God says to us". I began to wonder if I was possessed by the Devil.

Tom reiterated that Satan had been "defeated" on the cross, but what this means is unclear. The primary purpose of Jesus's death on the cross was, we had been repeatedly told, to absolve the world of its sins. Presumably, then, if the Devil's aim was to prevent us from reaching heaven, Jesus had created a route there that negated those Mephistophelean stratagems. But was the Devil "defeated" in the sense of losing power? If the negative effects of his work are to be seen in earthly suffering, he seems to be doing fairly well for himself on this plane. Even in the spiritual realm the prognosis doesn't look altogether good. After Jesus's great victory and much "mopping up", Europe, at least, shifted dramatically toward sinful secular ways, presumably as a result of the Devil's temptations. Far more Europeans are now hell-bound than in the past. It was a strange kind of victory.

Of course, Christians are uniquely well-equipped for their battle. In Luke[12] Jesus grants authority to his followers over demons, which are reportedly "afraid of Jesus's name". In order to do battle with them, Paul wrote in Ephesians[13] that Christians would have to use a variety of metaphorical military equipment "from his own time". In the passage that evidently inspired Jonathan Aitken's "sword of truth" speech, and possibly a number of Dungeons and Dragons authors, Christian warriors are told to wear "the belt of truth", "the breastplate of righteousness", "the boots of the gospel of peace", "the shield of faith", "the helmet of salvation" while they wield "the sword of the spirit". Most of the interpretations placed on these are fairly obvious. Notably the "shield of faith" is the "opposite of cynicism and scepticism" and protects "the mind against doubt".

Tom himself had used the shield, he said, because most of his family was not Christian, and he needed an "effective defence" against people who are "waiting for an opportunity to say 'Look at that – there's a hypocrite'". Jesus fended off the Devil using the sword: "each time Satan came at him Jesus used the scripture". This was a lesson for his followers, who should quote scripture "whenever in doubt". For this reason, Tom said, learning chunks of the Bible is very useful.

With this armoury to hand, Christians "don't need to be scared" during the "spiritual warfare". They can be reassured by the "relative powerlessness" of the enemy who is "about to be wiped out" (we must assume he's been "about to be wiped out", just as the end of the world has been imminent, for two thousand years). In order to bring about his final defeat, "prayer should be a priority", but not just prayer – Christians should, we were finally told, be prepared to preach, heal the sick and cast out demons. "We all," Tom dramatically reassured us, "have the power."

First priority for the discussion group was colds. Bill had issued his usual earnest, "So, how is everybody?" and in a break with tradition he'd been answered: everybody was suffering.

"Well we've got a doctor right here!" exclaimed Pete, his comedic reflexes undimmed.

"You can't treat colds," said Dr Phillip, with his usual air – either embarrassment or boredom depending on how you looked at him. But that was no barrier to humour. "Procter and Gamble have got a product though!" he said, grinning.

Sandy caught the comedy ball and told us about the new product at her company. "It's called 'First Defence'" she chuckled, pausing for that heartbeat which separates the hilarious from the merely funny, "but we've all got colds!" The group guffawed at the sheer gob-smacking irony of it all. Then we turned to the more serious matters of satanic influences.

The group seemed a little puzzled by the subject – was the occult really so dangerous? Anne led us into the subject with the example of her own dabblings. "You'll all look down your noses at me," she began, drawing breath for a tremulous admission, "but I went shopping at 'Think Again'." "Think Again" was a local "holistic" gift shop that sold energy crystals and books by the Dalai Lama. The group seemed unimpressed. "But I think it's sort of OK because all the occult stuff is on one side and all the stuff I want, the earrings and pretty pink things, are on the other." This seemed dubious: shouldn't she destroy her earrings and pretty pink things? Hadn't she patronised Satan's emporium and funded his wicked operations?

Generally the group didn't follow this hard line, partly, it seemed, because they didn't know what the shop sold. We were told it was "New Age". "What do they sell there?" asked Wilma.

"It's sort of Wicca and stuff," said Anne.

"Oh," said Wilma.

"Hang on… when you said Wicca, I was thinking of my furniture – I sit on that!" said Nadine, exploding into giggles.

"Hey hey – you'll have to throw that out!" bantered Pete.

Wilma was keeping her eye on the subject. "But shouldn't you know your enemy?" she asked.

"Yeah, surely a Christian should be able to read the occult and not be converted to it?" said Pete.

"Sometimes associating with the wrong people can turn you into one of them," Bill warned.

"What happens when you take this path? Do you end up being possessed by demons?" I wanted to know.

As usual I didn't get a straight answer. He allowed the others to laugh at the thought, although of course we'd just heard in the talk that the Devil commanded a formidable demonic army, and that Christians would need to fight them. In the end he threw back his head and evasively said, "There's been a lot of debate about this, about demonic influence versus possession." He wasn't going to be drawn on which he backed, but two weeks later was to reveal he had actually encountered and helped exorcise demons. The Alpha Course manual was also clear: demons did exist and possess people. It was just a question of how it happened, about which we'd only had hints. What was the mechanism? How did it begin with reading a horoscope and end in subservience to the Lord of Darkness?

And there was another interesting question, which Malc put to him: "Is there a difference between New Age beliefs and other religions? Should we consider other religions as the work of the Devil also?"

"That's a good question," answered Bill, not hurrying toward an answer.

It was deflected by Dr Phillip, who waffled about a pamphlet on Islam he'd seen, and Wilma, whom I began to suspect was a very cunning shill when she leapt in with, "I'm not really sure what New Age is". It was explained in vague terms and we moved on.

"If we should throw out and destroy all materials related to these occult practices, should we throw out a newspaper with a horoscope in it? Or not buy one?" I asked. Bill sat back and grinned, seeming to imply with his facial gestures that we should seriously consider it, sparking a debate on which newspapers were safe if this was the case.

Anne warned that her "school has been taken over by tarot reading, which is the 'next step' after astrology."

"But what does it lead to? Human sacrifice?" I asked

"When you move on to tarot that's when you can do it for yourself, that's when you use a demonic influence". I wondered why astrologers bothered convoking demons when their predictions were always so hazy and at variance with each other. The alternative explanation – that they in fact cobbled together collections of vague stock sentences – seemed more plausible, except that didn't square with the dangers their output evidently posed.

The group still wasn't convinced that astrology was hazardous.

"Well let me ask you this: How does a fisherman catch a fish?" Bill gnomically inquired, tipping his head back. "He throws out a line!" he triumphantly supplied, reeling in an imaginary fishing line with his hands as his head lurched forward. "You put bait out there and it gets you hooked", he continued, as the group looked on. He explained that if one's faith was strong enough one might be OK, but if not – well, the consequences were literally hellish. He talked again of the dark possibilities if one mixed with the wrong sort of person.

As usual Bill had a personal experience to share, this time related to a friend who'd been interested in the occult. (Interest in the occult and the satanic typically clusters around its sternest enemies, Christians. The Devil should review his tactics.) Bill's friend was very intellectual, and the last person you would have expected to be into the occult but "he had some stories to tell!" Unfortunately Bill couldn't actually tell us what these stories were because they were too awful. Luckily, his friend had since given up the occult and returned to Christianity and "you would never have known he was into witchcraft".

As the group mulled this compelling tale, Malc posed a key theological conundrum: "One thing I find strange is, if God created everything then he also created the Devil – why do that?"

Anne was waiting with a stock response "Because he wanted to give us free will."

"Isn't the Devil sin?" asked Pete.

"No," said Bill in one of his rare straight answers. This was consistent with Tom's talk. The Devil wasn't sin himself; he simply diverted Christians towards sin with his temptations. He was, we had to remember, a person, not a force.

"I understand that God gave us free will," I replied to Anne, "but the Devil makes things worse, right? I mean, he's responsible for all this suffering and misery we heard about in the talk. So why not kill him?"

"Well if we didn't have sin we wouldn't have free will," persisted Anne.

"But I understood that sin was separate from the Devil. In the talk they said we couldn't even blame sin on the Devil – it was our fault: he just tempted us and we gave in to temptation. But the Devil is apparently causing all these wars and so on via this temptation. So if we got rid of him we'd have a net reduction in sin, right? We could still be tempted, so we'd still have free will, but we'd have less temptation, so less sin and less suffering, surely?"

"But then we wouldn't have free will," replied Anne. I gave up.

Bill suggested God didn't act that way. I replied that he wasn't shy of striking down vast numbers of people in the Bible, so why not this one creature who caused such trouble? No answer came. Bill and the others seemed to view this questioning of God's tactics as in some way sacrilegious.

"There's definitely evil in the world and in my life," mused Pete. "It feels like we've come to a gunfight with a knife!"

"You think so?" asked Bill.

"Oh yeah. The Devil and his demons seem to be working very hard whereas God and his angels – they're just sitting back!"

Bill mumbled a vague reply so I made one last, futile attempt to get an answer to a question: "Why if the Devil has been defeated is he still so powerful? He seems to be causing more wars and suffering than ever." The response was a unique Bill shrug that somehow implied that the answer was an irrelevance. So instead we sat in silence until something else came up. As ever, Wilma supplied it.

"What about Harry Potter," she asked, focusing in on the crucial issue of our times. Anne gigglingly revealed that she'd read it, but "only as a story". How else she could have read it wasn't made clear – as a practical guide to sorcery? – but she was confident her strong faith had insulated her from its occult power. Why had the Pope bothered condemning it? It was for children's sake, Bill felt: it was dangerous if it popularised magic in their impressionable minds.

"How about *The Da Vinci* Code?" asked Malc. "I saw a book on the stall outside. Why is there this fuss about it? Surely people recognize it's just a novel?"

Bill suddenly became animated. "The problem I have with that guy," he began, stabbing his finger, "is that he says that everything in the book is true, and he's woven a story through it. He relies on some very bad popular scholarship." In spite of this vehement reaction, Anne couldn't help telling us she'd again dabbled in the occult and risked Dan Brown's temptations. Malc pointed out that she had quite an occult interest, given her reading and shopping choices. She laughed, confident the Boots of the Gospel of Peace were protecting her.

"Is Dan Brown under the influence of the Devil?" Malc inquired.

"A good question," said Bill, for what seemed the hundredth time. "Perhaps a topic for the group to discuss?" he suggested, looking round. But the discussion meandered instead on to the *The Last Temptation of Christ* (which Bill wasn't very much against, as it showed Jesus resisting the temptations of the flesh, however luridly they might have been portrayed). Inevitably *The Passion of the Christ* came up, which Bill also liked. When it was pointed out that many of the brutal details were not from the Gospels but from the visions of a German nun named Anne Catherine Emmerich, he demurred; he felt it was very true to reality.

After some more film criticism Bill moved to wind up the meeting. Before he did, I had to find how close to hell I really was. "All this stuff about the Devil causing doubt and scepticism – I find it a bit accusatory. Am I possessed by the Devil?"

"I'm moving away from you!" joked Pete. People laughed, but the idea didn't seem altogether absurd to the group.

Bill said honest questioning was OK but I still wasn't clear where the line was drawn. When did "honest questioning" morph into Luciferian scepticism? Nadine said her husband's grandfather hadn't even believed in the resurrection. This reminded Bill of a former bishop with wishy-washy beliefs: "He should never have been allowed near a pulpit." He told us a joke to end the session, about how the Devil and his demons were seeking to undermine Christianity. First they'd said Jesus wasn't the Son of God, and that had worked for a while. Then they'd said God didn't exist, but that too hadn't completely succeeded. Then they'd hit on a new slogan that worked brilliantly: "It doesn't matter!"

After that, Bill closed the discussion and we left for the pub. As we walked past "Think Again" Pete mentioned he'd been speaking to someone who thought reflexology was demonic. He wasn't happy: "I mean what are you supposed to do if you have sore feet? You can't have reflexology? What can you do?" At the pub his concern was the fruit flies. "I can't stand these bar flies!"

Another group leader called Carol appeared, and we talked about how the groups were going. Pete was worried that, unlike ours, her group began and ended with a prayer – they were all fully committed. He thought perhaps it was easier to persuade people with no background in Christianity. He admitted he'd almost given up after the Holy Spirit weekend, where he hadn't felt anything despite really hoping.

Carol murmured sympathetically. She reassured us that every group was different, and we shouldn't feel bad about not so far achieving a radical change. She'd had similar troubles at Bible Camp when she was twelve, but the next day after a spiritually difficult night in a tent she "felt a light coming on" (she made a lighter motion with her hand) and all was well. She clearly viewed it as inevitable that something similar would happen to us – sooner or later, if we tried hard enough, we'd find Jesus. As if to prove her point by the power of sheer love, as we left she hugged and kissed Pete and Malc – while I escaped down the road.

Notes

1. *Questions of Life*, p.157.
2. *How to Run the Alpha Course.*
3. Job 1:12.
4. See Chapter 4 and Appendix B.
5. Sprenger, J. & Kramer, H. *The Malleus Maleficarum.* 1978 Edition, Translated by Summers, M., Dover Publications Inc., London.
6. Apparently "they have slippery tongues, and are unable to conceal from the fellow-women those things which by evil arts they know; and, since they are weak, they find an easy and secret manner of vindicating themselves by witchcraft". Unfortunately woman is "more carnal than a man, as is clear from her many carnal abominations".
7. E.g. Joshua 10:1.
8. In Genesis 19:6-8 Lot offers his virgin daughters, in place of more esteemed male guests, to a gang of Sodomite rapists, saying, "Let me bring them out to you, and you can do what you like with them. But don't do anything to these men, for they have come under the protection of my roof." He received no punishment for this, but his wife was shortly thereafter turned into a pillar of salt for disobeying orders against looking at Sodom as they fled. God also famously instructed Abraham in Genesis 22 to kill his son Isaac and present him as a burnt offering. Abraham's willingness to cooperate was applauded.
9. Justified by Acts 19:19: "A number who had practised sorcery brought their scrolls together and burned them publicly."
10. There is no Biblical evidence that the concept of Satan existed in Jewish thought until much later. The tempter in the Garden of Eden was a "serpent", only later pronounced to be Satan.
11. Matthew 4:3: "The tempter came to him and said, 'If you are the Son of God, tell these stones to become bread.'" Matthew 4:6: "'If you are the Son of God,' he said, 'throw yourself down. For it is written: 'He will command his angels concerning you and they will lift you up in their hands, so that you will not strike your foot against a stone.'".
12. Luke 10:17-20.
13. Ephesians 6:11-17. Note that Paul's authorship of Ephesians is in doubt.

CHAPTER 12

Don't tell anyone or I'll be excommunicated

By now Alpha course goers were assumed to have been converted. There was no other way to interpret the title of this week's session, "Why and How Should We Tell Others?", unless the organizers expected unbelievers to spread the word. Still, I was keen to find how any Christian, given their lack of answers to the difficult questions, could be certain enough in their faith to tell others that it was The Truth.

After securing helpings of gelatinous stew we sat down with Anne, Pete and friends. Anne had had a difficult day in a classroom practising to be a teacher. The rules were getting her down: she wasn't allowed to cuddle or hit the children, or even put a plaster on a hurt knee. There was no way to discipline them. "Sometimes I think they need a good walloping," she said. Pete knew all about caning. One teacher at his school liked to throw a die and give that number of strokes. Worse, his mother's punishment for a caning at school was another caning.

On the upside, Anne's unruly classroom had supplied her with plenty of amusing stories. While writing the nativity story they'd produced some "Children say the funniest things!" gems – leopards watching over the infant Jesus, Joseph and Mary going to Bethlehem to pay for a taxi. This was all, of course, much less plausible than, say, a crucified man coming back from the dead three days after zombies burst from their graves.[1]

As we chatted, Dale Winton look-alike Jarvis arrived. His progress from the door had been accompanied by tittering and exaggerated concern from Pete's circle. Jarvis, it turned out, was "a bit of character", who caused outrage and amusement wherever he went. He soon illustrated his chaotic zaniness by revealing a stolen name badge with "Regina" on it and spilling a cup of coffee.

At our end of the table conversation turned to Catholicism. Malc mentioned that he'd been surprised to discover that the Inquisition still existed in renamed form ("The Congregation for the Doctrine of the Faith" – previously run by Pope Benedict XVI). Paul and Anne, both ex-Catholics, were more concerned with Mass. They found it strange that it was denied to non-Catholics. "But how would they know if you weren't a Catholic?" asked Pete. We shrugged. "How would they know though?" he asked again.

Anne revealed some personal history. Her partner Tod's parents were Jehovah's Witnesses. Tod's mother, disapproving of Anne, had "tried to scare" her. Anne had fertility problems, so Tod's mother had pointedly announced IVF was banned. Usually, Anne told us, her "faith was strong enough" to deal with this unpleasantness, but she'd been reduced to tears on occasion. It didn't seem right to probe further. She seemed a warm, open person, unwilling to confront the negative side of religious dogma. She said she'd thought of starting her own Alpha Course at her college. It was apparently easy to obtain the videos and so on, although she wasn't very confident about her abilities to lead it. She was certain, however, that she could do better jokes.

Pete announced that he'd had a look at the notorious "Think Again" shop. This prompted Anne to share a new opinion regarding astrology. Far from demonic influences, she now saw physics behind it. "Don't tell anyone or I'll be excommunicated," she giggled conspiratorially. "But I do think the moon has an effect on our behaviour. I mean we're made of 70% water, so it's like the tides. I do believe God created the moon, but it must have an effect." There wasn't a chance to follow up on this intriguing switch in her views. Or had this always been her view? Had she just followed the party line in the discussion the previous week?

As people sat down, Mike called up a satisfied customer who'd spoke to him earlier. I thought perhaps he'd tell us he'd had a miraculous experience with the Holy Spirit and been instantly converted. In fact he'd been looking at the Gumbel Bible reading guide, *Thirty Days*, and had been "so impressed". Since then he'd been handing them out to everybody, giving "one to my mum, one to my whole family". It was, he said, "a very, very, very powerful book."

At every session we'd been strongly encouraged to "grab some books", even if we didn't want to pay for them. As well as Alpha texts like *Thirty Days*, there were other on-message classics like *The Cross and the Switchblade* and C.S.Lewis's *Mere Christianity*. This reading material had two key traits. It presented a narrow, particular view of Christianity; and it made overt many of the hard line rules only hinted at in the sessions themselves. If they hadn't investigated elsewhere, a reader would come away from Mike's book table with a Charismatic, literalist conception of Christianity complete with various hard-line elements not featured in the main course, particularly in the area of sexual morality. If the Alpha course was actually about "exploring the meaning of life", as the banner outside still said, and if it really was an introduction to "basic" Christianity, why were course goers not encouraged to consider a variety of Christian standpoints, let alone those outside the faith? Why wasn't there a single book on offer written from a liberal theological perspective?

It seems fairly clear that the idea is to present an unthreatening, reasonable, positive view of Christianity in the talks and discussions, to attract the unsure. Once drawn in by the apparent openness and friendliness, people convince themselves, via these books, that to be a true Christian they must condemn homosexuality, refrain from extra-marital sex, and so on. The *Thirty Days* fan was well on his way, having pre-empted today's message by spreading the word among his family.

Tom knew his audience. "What do we do now?" he asked, cheekily, as a he strode onstage. "Oh… that's right – a true story!" The "true story" was about Jo and Laura, two "very posh" girls. As Tom gave these names, two female members of his flock in the front row dissolved into giggles, one of them resting her head on the other's lap as she shook with laughter. Being so very posh they'd gone hunting in Windsor Great Park, where Jo had suddenly fallen dangerously ill and apparently died. Laura had phoned Mike for help, and he'd started by telling her to make sure Jo was dead. He then heard the sound of a shotgun, followed by Laura asking, "What do I do next?"

As the chortling died down, Mike took the stand again. He had lots of facts and stories to illustrate why preaching was so important. He also had some anecdotes showing it all going wrong. On the positive side was a car dealer who'd excitedly questioned Mike about his faith when he'd learned his customer was a vicar. On the downside was a "bird man" preacher, who'd flown through the air with a loudhailer screaming the Christian message. And there was the pushy Evangelical who'd refused to recognize that Mike was a curate at the local church, instead persisting in his efforts to get him to their gathering where he could find out about Jesus. Anyone trying to lead the unfaithful to the Lord should try "not to be seen as a Bible Basher", so one shouldn't go "knocking on doors" or sounding like "American TV evangelists" – the key was "sensitivity". Mike had refused to wear a loud orange "mission" t-shirt when on a missionary course for these reasons.

In spite of these dangers, it was important to alert unbelievers to Jesus's great sacrifice because it's "selfish if you don't tell them". They need to be told because this is "not a secular country" and there is "a desperate need to hear the good news". Although he stressed that "it's not about numbers", Mike felt this was illustrated by declining church attendance (his own church was joyfully "bucking the trend"). During the "Welsh revival" early in the twentieth century a new church had appeared every eight days. By contrast, sixteen churches had closed in 2000. The "Decade of Evangelism" in the nineties had been a "flop" (church attendance had dramatically declined), and maybe, Mike suggested, we needed to ask if the church was "failing". If it was, the solution seemed to be Alpha course attendees permeating the world, promoting Nicky Gumbel's brand of Charismatic Christianity.

As usual, the methods had been shoehorned into a mnemonic scheme, each word beginning with a "P". The first was "presence". This boiled down to being nice upstanding people who led by example. For instance, Mike had had a profound effect on his colleagues, he said, by not swearing. As well as leading godly lives, Christians should be "speaking out in local government, on moral issues, on world issues". By doing so they would "preserve goodness in society" and secure "what's best for everyone". It was interesting that the personal sort of faith apparently assumed by most of our discussion group was being edged towards making a political stand. Naturally these moral examples would only lead unbelievers to God if they knew they emanated from Christians, so it entailed them being open about their faith. The question was: "Do people know you're a Christian?" Was it, Mike asked rhetorically, "just a private matter?" The answer was a strong no.

It seems obvious from the United States where Evangelical Christian involvement in politics leads. While a new convert who'd just read *Searching Issues* might not start waving a "God Hates Fags" placard (Alpha promotes "understanding" of their predicament while prohibiting their sex lives), they presumably would, for instance, campaign against homosexual vicars, for sexual abstinence, for the "sanctity of life" and its attendant policy implications, and so on. Gumbel does not spell out the implications, but he is clear about the need for Christian influence: "We are called as Christians to stop society going bad." Alpha followers must use their "influence to bring about God's standards in society". Apparently this entails "working for justice, freedom and dignity for the individual, and... helping to abolish discrimination" (just not for gay people).[2]

The second "P" was "persuasion". The most common objection to becoming Christian, Mike told us, was not wishing to change one's lifestyle to accommodate, for instance, abstinence from pre-marital sex. But there were, he conceded, occasions where non-believers had "genuine objections and questions", such as "What about other religions?" or "How can a god of love allow suffering?" In this case Christians must answer them. I had been trying for weeks to extract answers to these questions. In spite of his two theology degrees, to which he unfailingly alerted us, Bill had systematically avoided answering them. His assistants Sandy or Anne hadn't done any better. So what hope was there for someone without their training?

Thirdly there was "proclamation". While this could mean preaching, Mike conceded that "not everyone would like to stand here and do what I'm doing". Instead, a devout Christian could just persuade a wavering friend to attend a service to hear someone else. As Mike put it, "there's actually no greater privilege than actually bringing someone else to Christianity".

Mike and Gumbel's showpiece was the farmer who persuaded a young womanizing Billy Graham to drive his truck to Church services, setting him on the road to worldwide evangelism. "We can't all be like Billy Graham," Gumbel says, but that's perhaps not such a loss given Billy Graham's less marketable aspects. As with so many of Gumbel's exemplary figures, it seems as if almost any earthly crime can be excused by work directed at the heavenly realm. A recent unauthorized biography provides a staggering catalogue of the former that cannot be reproduced here.[3] A few examples of his Christian counsel are worth noting, however.

In 1972 Graham piously hoped, in conversation with Richard Nixon, that they might be able to "do something" about the Jews' "stranglehold" over America to avoid the country "going down the drain".[4] In 1969 he sent Nixon a memo urging bombing of North Vietnamese dikes. The likely outcome, according to US government estimates, was the loss of a million lives, but these were ungodly communist lives, and the idea originated from Christian missionaries, so this was presumably just another in a long line of divinely-sanctioned genocides.[5] In 1991 Graham was still guiding the presidency, this time with the insight that Saddam Hussein was "the Antichrist itself".[6] It also turns out that the preacher Graham was so happily encouraged to see in Gumbel's anecdote was Mordecai Ham, a man renowned for "anti-Semitic rantings and racist slurs".[7] But "Billy Graham has led thousands to faith in Christ", so why would these things be worth consideration or mention?[8]

The other side of "proclamation" was "explaining ourselves"— "sharing our faith". Mike said unbelievers were often fascinated by Christians' journeys to faith, so one should tell them about it: "people like a personal story". In the manual was a handy appendix advising faith sharers to "make it short", "make it personal" and "keep it Christ centred".

The most mysterious of the methods was "power", presumably in the same sense as Nicky Gumbel's hero John Wimber used it in his books *Power Evangelism*, *Power Healing* and *Power Points*.[9] The Alpha manual says, referring to Acts 3, that "a miracle arouses great interest", but it wasn't made clear what we should do about it. Could we expect to perform miracles? This wasn't stated, but if not why raise the subject? As so often, the implication was of something nobody was keen to enunciate explicitly.

Finally we had "prayer". Mike summarized the situation by saying we should "direct people to Jesus, and actually pray for them, and actually let Jesus into their hearts". He mentioned an incident where he'd been praying for a damaged individual in need of help and suddenly felt "a strong urge – a really, really strong urge – to tell him

God loved him". The man started crying, saying "I'm a road sweeper – I clean up other people's mess. Nobody loves me." Prayer was the key, because without it failure was inevitable, for it isn't possible for a Christian to convert anybody – only God could do that. Mike ended with the comment, "Jesus is actually worth sharing".

Most of the group seemed in good spirits, although Bill said he was tired and spent almost all his time slouched nearly horizontal, an arm draped over the back of his chair. His first interest was Belinda's tracksuit: "You're looking a bit sporty! Have you been to the gym?" She explained she'd just been walking the dog, and then lapsed into silence for the rest of the session.

Wilma opened the discussion by saying that she had found Mike's anecdote about the Evangelical trying to convert him in the street "amusing". She went on to add that she didn't really know what Evangelical meant but she was sure that this Church was getting more Evangelical and wasn't as traditional as it used to be. She was very concerned about neglect of The Book of Common Prayer. She thought it might put people off the church.

"Well, whole theses have been written about what Evangelical means!" Bill said. He then launched into a story about a "very clever guy who was a lecturer" who hated using the term "Evangelical". Bill stressed it was a personal view, but he was all for the church becoming more "happy clappy". He and Sandy pointed out that there were traditional services at 9.15 am every Sunday, but the Wilma felt that this wasn't an attractive time. She repeated that she thought people would feel uncomfortable at the new style services. They meandered around the topic for a while, with Bill using the analogy of going into a betting shop ("I wouldn't know what to do!"). Sandy revealed that she always bet on the Grand National.

"Is gambling actually disapproved of in the Bible?" Malc asked. The only answer was a giggling admission from Anne that she gambled too. Malc replied, "You're just a hard drinking, hard gambling occultist at heart aren't you?" eliciting more embarrassed giggling.

(The Bible does not specifically prohibit gambling. Those arguing against it tend to point to passages like 2 Thessalonians 3:10: "For even when we were with you, we gave you this rule: 'If a man will not work, he shall not eat.'" Supposedly gambling is contrary to this biblical injunction that one should acquire money via honest toil. Undercutting Paul's pronouncement here about living off others, however, are other passages regarding slavery. Colossians 3:22, for instance, has this to say: "Slaves, obey your earthly masters in everything; and do it, not only when their eye is on you and to win their favor, but with sincerity of heart and reverence for the Lord."[10])

There was a lull in the conversation until Bill said, "so has anybody got any evangelical stories of their own to tell?"

"I can make one up!" exclaimed Pete. But we found he wasn't actually keen to, so Bill stepped into the breach. He'd known a man named "Chipper" in the air force – "a real livewire" – who knew almost nothing of Christianity except for a couple of the miracle stories. Bill had been talking to him one day about Christianity and the difficulty "of developing a relationship with God". "It's like you keep trying to build bridges to God and they keep getting knocked down," he'd said.

He hadn't been prepared for Chipper's reply: "Oh it's like that story about Jesus walking on water – like he was trying to come to us because we couldn't go to him".

A beatific grin spread on Bill's face as he described his response: "I don't know what's going on here, but I'm listening!" He'd been "blown away" by this powerful analogy from an untutored gadabout, the moral seemingly that you could hear about Jesus from the most unlikely sources.

Then we moved on to more serious matters. Malc said, "I find it odd that this session was included in the Alpha course, because even if I'd been converted to Christianity and wanted to tell others it would be very difficult for me, because I'm still not sure what it is be a Christian. We haven't even agreed on what a sin is." Sandy laughed. Bill nodded pensively.

Eventually Bill broke off his cogitative slouching and leaned forward, hands clasped, and announced, "It's a good question". He even seemed close to answering it, but Wilma had other concerns.

"It's not completely relevant," she admitted, "but I had this friend – a really nice man…" He'd been thoroughly nice, but his divorced wife had indoctrinated their children so that they repeatedly told him he'd go to hell. "What do you say to that?" she asked. "Do you think being moral and righteous is just being Christian?"

"Or is it the way we've been conditioned by society?" asked Bill, in mysterious lecturer mode. Nobody seemed to react. "Sorry for bringing up something so heavy!" he apologized. Remarkably, he then turned back to Malc's question, agreeing that the placing of this session in the course was strange. Sandy concurred. Realizing that a discussion with some relevance might break out in spite of her efforts, Wilma started to pack up, glancing at the clock.

"I have a kind of related question," I said. "There are these difficult questions mentioned in the manual – about suffering for instance. And it says Christians should try to get the answers before preaching. But, well, shouldn't they sort these out before believing – isn't it putting the cart before the horse? I haven't heard any answers myself."

"I don't think it's putting the cart before the horse," said Bill. "What is the question about suffering?" At this point Wilma barged out with a mumbled farewell, nearly knocking Sandy out with her handbag.

"I can't reconcile a loving god with the disasters that happen in the world. How can I believe he's loving when he does these things or allows them to happen?"

"You can view it like that, but in the Holocaust, some people had problems, but others actually had their faith strengthened by their experiences."

"But I'm talking about the world as a whole, not personal views. We have this loving God, and he lets all these people suffer and die. Why?"

Sandy thought God had helped us cope with disasters by providing technology. She mentioned the 2004 Christmas tsunami. If the devastated areas had been Christian, she implied, they would have implemented a tsunami warning system. Bill weighed in with another example of where humans could do more to help themselves – this time it was Vesuvius. He wasn't happy with the roads around that volcano: "The only escape route is a dual carriageway, and when it erupts, you know what'll happen." He slapped his fist into his hand.

"OK, so in some circumstances God has allowed us to alleviate the effects of these things, but there are plenty of cases where there was nothing that could have been done. Why did he allow these disasters to happen?"

Anne was keen to flourish her favourite response. "I think it's down to free will," she began, apparently before thinking through how. Eventually she suggested God would step in more if we were godlier. Bill nodded.

"Are you saying there would be fewer natural disasters if the world was Christian?"

Bill backed away from this, indicating that things would be better but only in some indistinct sense. Nadine seemed to be on his side. She found it awfully funny that the "mad Mullahs" had attributed Hurricane Katrina to Allah's wrath but had kept silent about the earthquake in Pakistan.

I pointed out that religious leaders of all types frequently claim to know the reason behind disasters, including Hurricane Katrina, which was variously blamed on homosexuals, Israel's withdrawal from Gaza, abortion, US policy in Iraq, and witchcraft. Surely the key issue was whether, if God had any influence on these matters, we could discern who was getting the help. As it was, nobody could point to any compelling evidence for their god's intervention.

This didn't stop Anne claiming that prayer could indeed help with such problems. But she didn't make it clear what the effect would be; instead she diverged onto a strange analogy involving Tony Blair's policy on nuclear power, the clear implication being that it was wrong. "That's very political," admonished Sandy. Anne apologized.

Then Pete came up with another standard justification for earthly suffering: "But isn't the point that it's not what happens in this word but the next one – isn't that what we're preparing for?"

That theory might fly, except it was inconsistent with a great deal of what we'd heard in the course. Of course we'd been assured our souls were in need of a saviour. But the first reason given for listening to the Alpha message was the great void in our lives in this material world. The numerous everyday examples of God's work explicitly pointed to his intervention in this life. If the rewards of Christianity were all in heaven what was prayer-based "healing" (next week's topic) all about?

I put this to Pete: "Well, OK, but if that's the case then why did we hear about God intervening in people's lives, and helping them choose houses, and so on? If he intervenes to that extent, why not do more serious things, like save thousands of people from dying under the rubble of their houses?" Pete shrugged as if the question had never interested him particularly in the first place, and the discussion ended there.

As we got up to leave, Pete asked people if they wanted to come to Hillsong, delivering his usual "extreme sports" description. Unfortunately he focused on the pushy donations practices (an envelope on each seat), perhaps putting people off. Wilma immediately said, "Oh no, I don't think so." Dr Phillip and his wife were vehemently uninterested. Bill and Anne started to make excuses, but in the face of Pete's enthusiasm eventually agreed to come. We were set, then, for an extreme tongues experience in the presence of Alpha believers.

Notes

1. According to Matthew, a zombie invasion occurred when Jesus died on the cross – 27:52-53: "The tombs broke open and the bodies of many holy people who had died were raised to life. They came out of the tombs, and after Jesus' resurrection they went into the holy city and appeared to many people."
2. *Questions of Life*, p.175-176.
3. Bothwell, C (2007). *Prince of War: Billy Graham's Crusade for a Wholly Christian Empire*. Brave Ulysses Books.
4. Ibid., p.125-126.
5. Ibid., p.109-110.
6. Ibid., p.167.
7. Martin, W. (1991). *A Prophet With Honor: The Billy Graham Story*. Quill. New York, p.63.
8. *Questions of Life*, p.181.
9. Wimber J. (2001). Power Evangelism. Hodder Headline; Wimber, J. (1991). Power Healing. Harper One; Wimber, J. (1991). Power Points: Your Action Plan to: Hear God's Voice, Believe God's World, Seek the Father, Submit to Christ, Take Up the Cross, Depend on the Holy Spirit, HarperCollins.
10. 1 Corinthians also makes plain this indulgent view of slave ownership in 7:20-24: "Each one should remain in the situation which he was in when God called him. Were you a slave when called? Don't let it trouble you – although if you can gain your freedom, do so. For he who was a slave when he was called by the Lord is the Lord's freedman; similarly he who was a free man when he was called is Christ's slave. You were bought at a price; do not become slaves of men. Brothers, each man, as responsible to God, should remain in the situation God called him to." Other translations like to render "slaves" here as "servants", although the reference was definitely to slaves. These passages were used by anti-abolitionists to justify slavery in the American Civil War.

CHAPTER 13

The Extreme Sports of Churchgoing

The trip to see Hillsong revealed a clear divide in our group. Pete and Bill were keen, and so apparently was Anne, although her mother told us on the day that she couldn't make it. Nobody else was remotely interested in the extreme sports of churchgoing. The prospect seemed to horrify Sandy.

Pete offered his people-carrier, so I hitched a lift with him and Bill to the Leatherhead Hillsong franchise. Malc was to meet us there. Pete found the whole idea of the trip hilarious, and kept grinning as we prepared to set off. On the way he mentioned George Best's death. This moved Bill to mention his history working with alcoholics. He regretted not being able to continue this – apparently there weren't enough in the locality.

Pete was keen to pull the conversation back to Hillsong.

"Are you looking forward to it, Stuart?" he asked, chuckling.

"Well, I'm sure it's going to be interesting. I'm intrigued to see what this extreme worship is like."

"Oh, it's extreme all right!" Pete guffawed.

"Yeah, well I can't imagine what sort of form it could take, so that'll be interesting…"

"It's EXTREME."

"I'd still like to see HTB – maybe we can do that – but this definitely sounds the most interesting."

Bill told me he went to HTB every week. He seemed keen to organize a visit, although I couldn't quite see why – did he think it had something new to offer?

"I was wondering, actually… I was reading a book about another church in London. It was called the 'London Healing Mission', run by Andy Arbuthnot, I think…"

"I haven't heard of that particular church."

The book in question was titled "All You Need is More and More of Jesus", and Arbuthnot was an Anglican clergyman.[1] It turned out, though, that Arbuthnot's prescription for a number of female congregationists was actually Holy Dubonnet and crucifixes applied to various orifices in lengthy naked sessions in a soundproof room. He termed these procedures "internal ministries", and was aided in them by his wife. It was necessary, he said, to exorcise demonically possessed genitals arising from Satanist parents. Even after his arrest and defrocking, Arbuthnot insisted that his approach to spiritual warfare was unexceptionable.[2]

An extreme case? No doubt. But if one believes in the reality of demonic forces, as Alpha attendees are encouraged to do, then it is not entirely surprising when one lands up at bizarre medieval beliefs reminiscent of *Malleus Maleficarum*, because the underlying supernatural premise is the same.[3] If people are vulnerable to demons then clearly their genitals are at risk. If they are possessed by the negation of all that is good and holy, is prayer enough? Add the arbitrary power granted by a supposed hotline to God (Arbuthnot's ministrations were guided by prayer), and it is surprising that there is not more of this kind of thing.

"What I found interesting was he seemed to deal with demons a lot. After the week on how to resist evil I was really intrigued… I was wondering, have you had any experiences with demons?"

"Not many, no…"

"You have encountered them?"

"There was once, when I was studying, and I was doing a survey, asking people their views on Christianity. There was one man… I felt a cold presence."

"You were just asking people in the street about Christianity?"

"Yeah. And there was this one guy, and he just had this very arrogant attitude…"

"He was against Christianity?"

"He was… and it was just something – it's difficult to describe – it was a feeling I had. I don't say this lightly, but I've never felt this before. But when I spoke to him I just felt a chill across my soul."

"It must have been a pretty extreme experience…"

"Yeah!" said Pete, fervently. He seemed completely convinced of the existence of demons.

"It was," said Bill, apparently now enjoying his dramatic revelation.

"So you think he might've been possessed?" I asked.

"I think it's possible. There was just something there."

"That's extraordinary."

We contemplated Bill's brush with Satan for a few seconds in silence, then Pete questioned Bill about his surveys and studying, and the conversation moved on. As we reached the outskirts of Leatherhead I felt I had to probe Bill further about the demonic plane. What were the practical measures he used to fight off these dark influences?

"I was wondering… the other thing I read about in that book I mentioned was exorcism. What's your view of that?"

Bill drew in breath, and considered the matter. He clearly felt this was a subject around which he had to be careful. "I think there's a lot of very dubious stuff that goes on…"

"Fake exorcisms?"

"You need to be very careful… but I have seen it happen…"

"You've done an exorcism yourself?"

"I haven't, but I was staying once at a conference, and a friend of mine – I helped him. I prayed."

"You helped him exorcise a demon?"

"There was someone who had a power in them…"

"They spoke in demonic voices?"

"That kind of thing…"

"Convulsions?"

"Yes."

"Wow, that's pretty heavy," said Pete.

"Your friend drove out the demon?"

"Yes."

He said this as we drew into the car park, so attention turned to finding the theatre Hillsong hired for their services. After walking past the beaming black-clad Hillsong helpers at the door, we entered a throng of young people in a foyer heavily stamped with the Hillsong brand. There were large presentation screens positioned all around the walls, newsletters and magazines on tables asking questions like "Hot Air or Holy Fire?", and a video screen showing Hillsong's greatest hits. Christian rock flowed out of speakers. The atmosphere was frenetic, almost menacingly upbeat.

Seeing a helper with a coffee jug, I queued for a drink. As I stood there, a volunteer wearing the regulation black t shirt button-holed me.

"Hi!" he exclaimed. His enthusiasm had me half-convinced I should know him from somewhere.

"Err... hi."

He thrust out a hand, and continued grinning, as if our meeting had turned a dreary day into something magical. We shook hands. I remained silent.

"Is this your first Hillsong?" he asked, after a moment, making it sound like the central event of one's life.

"Yes."

"What brought you along, then?" he asked, in a strong Australian accent. I realized that every helper I'd heard had had an Australian accent. Hillsong is based in Australia, but this still seemed slightly odd in Britain.

"I was just seeing what it was like really..." He looked a little disappointed. Then he brightened, spying another target behind me.

"Well, I hope you enjoy it!"

I returned to Bill and Pete. Soon enough there was an announcement that the service was beginning, and the coffee jugs were withdrawn. Malc hadn't arrived so we wandered in.

"Best get a seat near the door, eh, for when the bucket comes round?" said Paul.

We sat down at the end of a row near the back. The stage was dominated by a projector screen showing the Hillsong logo, with huge speakers either side emitting loud uplifting rock. We watched the place fill up. Most people looked below thirty, with a high proportion of families.

Soon enough the doors closed, the music became louder, and lights started flashing. A band reminiscent of *Busted* came out on stage. The background music dropped, and people stood up. The band launched into a repetitive, anthemic song that soon had many of the audience swaying their hands. I stood scanning the audience. They all seemed rapt, even if they weren't moving to the music. Bill was gazing intently at the stage.

Eventually, after several more songs, a bald man came out for what looked at first to be the sermon. He updated us on the prayer situation, with the "praise reports". Like a DJ doing shout-outs, he had slips of paper in his hand with details of successful prayer. It was important, he explained, to realize that a pay rise or a promotion or some other piece of luck was always God's work – and we must acknowledge it. (Bad events are of course far more complicated, usually indicative of human failings and always evidence that God wants what's best for us in the long term.)

Then he launched into a rambling exegesis of Malachi chapter 3, which it emerged was all about donating money to Hillsong. Ideally this would be in the form of "tithing" – that is, donating ten percent of one's income to the cause. If we didn't hand over enough money, the bald inquisitor informed us, we were effectively robbing the Lord. He told us in detail about how we should bring our donations "into the house of God", by which he meant we should hand over the begging envelopes on each seat. It was, he stressed, very easy to donate using credit cards; and we should consider "gift aid", so Hillsong could claim the tax. What neither he nor the envelopes disclosed was what the money was spent on.

After around ten minutes of exhortations he finally told us about the speaker. We were "very lucky", he emphasized repeatedly, to have Brian Houston himself talking to us – "one of the top speakers around", "one of the top leaders in the body of Christ". He was concerned there was a blasé attitude towards having the glorious Brian Houston, the leader of Hillsong, in person in the church. Then the buckets came round. We speedily passed them on.

I was wondering at this point where Malc had got to. It turned out he'd been detained outside the auditorium by earpiece-sporting bouncers. It wasn't polite, they'd explained, to interrupt the donation session. In fact they'd originally taken him for some lost theatregoer – clearly not church material – and barred his entry to the building. Once the bald exhorter had left the stage Malc was allowed in, just as the buckets were being collected. During this process we watched a youth TV-style church news video. The main subject was money.

Then it was time for more incantatory music from the band. As before, people pumped their fists and swayed, while Bill seemed to be reaching another plane altogether: he stood, head tipped back, eyes closed, singing along, possibly filled with the power of the Spirit.

Once the audience was pumped up Brian Houston bounced onto the stage. He took a rhythmic approach to sermonising, repeating over and over the same point with slightly different wording. The biblical message was leavened with jokes about youthful pranks and how Tim, the singer in the band (still on stage), used to steal his car. An apparent reformed violent criminal in the front row came in for some ribbing – a jocular testament to the reforming power of the Lord.

During this sermon Bill extracted his Bible from a battered metal case. He intently followed the quotations Houston cited, occasionally nodding. I pulled out my far larger Oxford Annotated Bible, to show I was serious. Other audience members took a more active approach, shouting "Yes!" and "That's right!" and "Amen!" whenever they felt particularly moved.

The theme was not being boxed. "Don't be boxed!" Brian kept yelling, waving his arms as he alternated between impassioned crescendos and hilarious in-jokes. He used the example of Jesus healing a blind man to suggest that Christians shouldn't be "boxed" by others' expectations. Such "boxing" was a strategy of the Devil. Despite its length, this was essentially all the content the sermon had. Eventually Houston ran out of different ways to say the same thing and called on Tim to take the stage.

Tim was clearly an expert at working the crowd, in spite of his youth. He didn't deliver a sermon, but, as the band strummed rhythmically in the background, built up to a tremulous, make-or-break moment. He addressed his words to each individual, asking them to think deeply, and consider if "it's your day today". Maybe, he suggested, it was the day when "you're prepared to make that commitment to Christ". If so, "raise your hands!" A couple of people did. Tim asked us to pray for these brave souls, and said their positions had been noted so Hillsong "hosts" could give them a useful book and track their progress.

But he wasn't satisfied, so we went round again. Again the band supplied a build-up. This was the moment, if we wanted to commit to

Christ, if we hadn't accepted Jesus, or if we had "backslid", this was the moment, now was the time to let him into our hearts. Again he got another couple of takers, and eventually the public affirmation session was over.

After some more crowd-pleasing music, the bald man (it emerged his named was Gary) was back, and not in a happy mood. "When you're here, you're guests," he told us. "And when you're a guest you follow the rules of the house where you're a guest, right? I don't think that's unreasonable – do you?" The problem was bozos. "I see bozos getting up and leaving during the sermon. That's just RUDE! Don't you think? I'm not being unreasonable am I?" He seemed furious.

"No!" screamed an audience member, provoking a ripple of "nos" through the audience.

He continued with his favourite "house of God" theme for several minutes. It was evidently convenient to refer to Hillsong as the "house of God" – it made anything it did irreproachable. "So if you see one of these bozos, just put your hands on their head, and say to them, 'Look, I'm sorry, but we don't do that here.'" He seemed deadly serious.

The ticking off finally over, the band started up again. It was time for something positive, so Gary asked us to take the hand of our neighbour. Malc stared straight ahead as the woman next to him lunged. Then, after a few more songs – all the songs were essentially one long chorus – we filed out past the *Friends* take-off on the video screen, to be treated to cookies and drinks, and browse the collection of inspiring books and DVDs. Houston was well-represented among these, along with numerous Hillsong CDs and DVDs and the works of people like Joel Osteen, a Christian self-help king with the aspect and slicked back hair of a second-hand car salesman. Very little of what was on offer seemed reflective or self-critical; it all seemed affirmative, positive, and very light on intellectual content – much like Hillsong.

Discussing the service over coffee, I found Pete and Bill didn't share my views. They agreed the atmosphere wasn't appropriate for every occasion, and Pete said he didn't view Hillsong as "a substitute for church", but they both felt that it was more than redeemed by the "joy of the spirit" on show.

Hillsong certainly comes across as a joyful place: everybody we saw looked happy. But even during a short visit some disturbing aspects were apparent. Few churches are so intent on policing of the congregation. Few are so fixated on money. Spontaneous affirmation of the Lord's bounty is allowed in many forms, but entering or leaving the service at one's convenience isn't. Pledging 10% of one's income to the church is a spiritual obligation, but Brian Houston's multi-million dollar properties, Breitling watch, etc. are his alone – the reward, apparently, that can be expected by anybody who has pleased God as much as he has.[4] He outlines "God's amazing financial plan for your life" in his book, *You need more money*. The amazing plan doesn't entail setting up a church that demands a tenth of its congregationists' income.

Notes

1. Arbuthnot, A. (1993). *All You Need is More and More of Jesus*. Highland Books.
2. Howard, R. (1997). *Charismania*. Mowbray. London. "Church warning on risks of exorcism", Andrew Brown, *Independent*, August 24th 1996.
3. See Chapter 11.
4. Hillsong's True Believers". *Sydney Morning Herald*, 7th November 2004.

CHAPTER 14

Why do Christians get colds?

The food this week was the most unappetising yet – strange sausage-like objects draped in brown sauce and diaphanous red cabbage. It reminded me of being at school. Nobody at the table finished their food. One woman went off to buy a kebab, which got her into trouble with a small girl collecting the plates. Pete seem to find the whole thing hilarious, maliciously asking, "Didn't feel hungry then, eh Stuart?" as my full plate was handed back.

Pete, Clive and Jo had a lengthy discussion about ironing. Pete liked to provoke: "My wife usually does it, but she's not very good at it, so I do it again. She does my shirts, and I tell her I'm going to have to do it again!"

"That's outrageous!" said Jo. "You're treading on thin ice!" said the kebab eater.

Jo was happy she wasn't eating much because she had to fit into a party dress – just grist for Pete's comedy mill. "I look good in a dress!" he said, grinning. Jo held her hand over her mouth in mock shock. "I didn't tell you I like wearing dresses!" he continued. Such japery in a church clearly ignored the solemn pronouncement in Deuteronomy 22:5 that cross-dressing is abhorrent to the Lord.

"Ooh, does your wife know about this?" Jo asked. The banter went on for some time like this. Then, after a thorough discussion of reality TV, the call came for the talk to begin.

Mike was absent, so Tom had to deliver the joke and the sermon. Mike had visited the doctor, saying, "I look terrible" – his hair was "wiry and frazzled" and his "eyes were popping out". The doctor turned to him and said, "Well Mike, there's nothing wrong with your eyesight!" The audience seemed more disappointed by the shortness than the content. It took a while before they realized the joke had finished. "Sorry, it was short notice," apologized Tom.

The subject was "Does God heal today?": "Now I have to admit I find this the hardest talk to give. The demons were bad enough, but this is harder! There's painful stuff here. And a lot of people approach it with fear and scepticism. So I'm just going to give the talk as it is in the book. There are good reasons to expect healing and they can have a really remarkable effect on people's lives – not just physically."

Of course there's plenty of divine healing in the Bible. God promised to heal his followers in Exodus,[1] although in the same sentence he also said that "no one shall miscarry or be barren in your land", which doesn't seem to have panned out. A similarly strong commitment in Psalms 41:3 claims that "the Lord will sustain him on his sickbed and restore him from his bed of illness". Gumbel is particularly taken with the example of Naamen,[2] who had his skin complaint cured when he bathed in a river at the Prophet Elisha's behest. Also cited is Isaiah 38, where King Hezekiah cures a boil with a lump of figs, possibly at divine instigation.

But the healing really gets underway in the New Testament, with Jesus. According to the manual, his healing work constitutes 25% of the Gospels, where he dealt with many types of illness as well as raising Lazarus from the dead.[3] "Clearly," said Tom, "no one had performed greater miracles than Jesus." This is at the least debatable – the Old Testament is filled with miracles on a grander scale than any in the new: Jesus only walked on water whereas Moses parted the sea. Anyhow, we were assured that healing had continued after Jesus's death when his apostles cured people in Acts.[4] Church fathers such as Irenaeus, Origen and Augustine also reported healing activity on their watch.

The talk swerved toward a far more metaphorical conception of healing, tied to salvation and the Apocalypse. "History," said Tom, "is moving towards this climax" – the second coming, helpfully illustrated by timelines in the manual showing where Jesus "broke into history". "History as we know it will end – that's in the future. For some who've turned away from Christ it's going to be bad – there's going to be destruction." The real healing will begin when Jesus returns, and that will happen soon.

Back on physical illness, Gumbel strains to promote the idea that Jesus handed over healing duties to all his disciples. One citation is from Matthew, but that doesn't mention healing, and refers only to Jesus commanding his eleven key disciples to spread the word.[5] Another plank of the case is in Matthew 10, where healing is mentioned, but again Jesus only instructs the twelve. Luke 10 is cited, but the authority granted in this passage to seventy disciples doesn't include straightforward healing; it relates to casting out demons and the ability to tread on snakes and scorpions without being hurt – not abilities claimed by most followers. John 14:12 has Jesus saying that "anyone who has faith in me will do what I have been doing". Exactly what that means isn't clear, but if it really is a blanket transfer of powers then turning water into wine would surely be common at Alpha events.

Finally, Gumbel turns to Mark 16:18,[6] where all disciples are explicitly told they will be healing the sick, but which he carefully describes as "good evidence of what the early church thought", rather than what Jesus said (the section purports to report Jesus's words). Gumbel says this because that part of Mark is not present in the earliest manuscripts, and is generally considered a later addition. Aside from healing, the verse has the resurrected Jesus handing over other remarkable abilities: believers will "pick up snakes in their hands, and if they drink any deadly thing, it will not hurt them" – a claim that led to the "Snake Handler" church founded by George Went Hensley, where interaction with rattlesnakes was advocated. The use of rattlesnakes understandably declined after Hensley died from a snake bite during a service in 1955.

In the light of all this healing from God, Tom informed us that we could be "so much more confident that he will act even more strongly today". Was this borne out by the evidence? There didn't, for instance, seem to be any reports of participants raised from the dead at Charismatic healing services. It seems undeniable that God's healing works have declined since Jesus's time. Of course, rational scrutiny has increased, but no doubt this is a coincidence.

We were now ready to tackle the crux of the sermon: how to heal nowadays using the power of the Lord. Since no instructions are given in the Bible, one must follow Jesus's example of "simplicity" and "love" by coupling sympathetic words with prayer. The Christian healer should consider why the illness exists, responding perhaps with the laying on of hands, or possibly – a personal touch from Tom, this – anointing with oil. The cause of the illness is particularly important because some ailments stem from a lack of forgiveness. Apparently a woman had forgiven the person who had injured her, and become "properly healed" after she dispatched a placatory letter. Another person had simply needed to place his faith in God before his unpleasant skin condition floated away in the bath.

Unfortunately God does not always step in. Sometimes people are not healed, and their Christian helper should not blame this on lack of faith. "There is nothing worse," said Tom, "than some idiot saying 'your faith is not strong enough.'" Christians should not always expect to have the healing power, because "the commission to heal isn't for everybody". As with tongues, there was seemingly no reason at all why good people should not have the gift – "we will see God at work, active in our lives" – and we should thank God, and attribute any marvellous healings to him; but if nothing happened, well, that wasn't anyone's fault. Tom ended the sermon with his characteristic "Here endeth the homily", spoken in a sardonic-sounding way that left me with the impression that he didn't quite buy into what he was saying.

It was a small discussion group this time, with only Pete, Bill, Dr Phillip and Sandy. The first subject up for discussion was Hillsong, which Sandy was keen to hear about. Pete enthused about the music again: "I really love the music – just great music". Bill was less keen on that, saying he preferred a service with more opportunity for reflection. He told us about an excellent music director he'd known at another church - "a clever guy" – who had unobtrusively woven together musical strands more varied than available at Hillsong. The group seemed to agree that Hillsong's breathlessly happy style wouldn't suit every mood. Pete re-emphasized the "great music".

"I found the guy asking for money, and telling people not to leave, a bit too aggressive," I said.

"Yeah," said Pete, "I thought the sermon was excellent – really good. But that guy, he said too much. I was looking round to see your reaction when he started talking about the money!"

Bill was of a similar mind. "I actually thought what he was saying about donating money was really good. But when he was talking about people leaving, I thought 'Say it once, that's fair enough', but when he just came back and said some more I just wanted him to shut up, to be honest." He didn't seem to think the laying of hands on bozos was constructive.

"The other thing was, I was a bit surprised when they asked people to put up their hands if they'd accepted Jesus – that they'd take their names, and give them books, and check on their progress. I was thinking some people would find that intimidating, and it could maybe discourage them."

Bill wasn't going to agree completely with that one. "I hear what you're saying – that could be true – but people making their walk in faith might need support." He seemed irked that everything I'd said about Hillsong had been negative. Sandy, on the other hand, found it all amusing, although I wasn't really sure why. Did she find the idea of Hillsong inherently funny? Or just someone like me going?

Once we'd covered Hillsong we turned to the matter at hand. "What did you think of the talk?" Bill asked the group at large.

"I thought it was good," said Pete. Silence reigned, as Bill nodded earnestly.

"I have a question," I began. "I was wondering… we heard all these stories about Christians being healed, so I'm wondering if Christians are healthier – can you see this healing in statistics?"

"Hmm, that's an interesting question," said Sandy. "Do Christians get less colds?"

"I think that would be too hard to find out," said Dr Phillip, flaunting his epidemiological knowledge. "The confounding factors would be too large. And you have these people who say they're Christian – a lot of people say they're Christian but they don't go to church."

"But the confounding factors surely aren't worse than in lots of other cases. If you're looking at the effect of living near pylons or whatever…I don't see why this is harder."[7]

"Ah, but what's a Christian?" asked Bill, enigmatically.

"Well, I agree there are some nominal Christians who maybe don't qualify, but surely you could go to a god-fearing town in America, in the Bible Belt, and just see if they have more healing – longer life expectancy – than other people in comparable circumstances?"

"I think they would live longer because they don't drink and things," said Dr Phillip.

"Yeah, I can believe that. But you have this with lots of medical trials don't you? You can surely try to account for those factors just as in other cases?"

"The problem," pronounced Bill, "is that you can't test God. He doesn't work that way." But how then to interpret Gumbel's inspiring tale in *A Life Worth Living*? He tells there how an ungodly tribe in the Philippines demanded proof from one of his missionary friends: "If Jesus was God they wanted to see him action". They "pushed forward a middle-aged man, blind from birth" and, of course, his sight was miraculously restored. Fifty people were converted and, "[t]he church there is still growing."[8] God sometimes can be tested, it seems – at least when the evidence looks positive.

"But I'm saying we've already got the statistical data. I mean, he didn't know when he did the healing that we'd look at the data already in existence"

"Ah," said Bill, "but he knows what happens in the future, so he WOULD know." He grinned.

"OK, I see what you're saying… but doesn't that imply that I could stop a group of people being healed just by threatening to test them?"

Bill stopped grinning, and adopted a more severe, professorial expression. "I think we're getting onto facile reasoning there," he admonished.

"Well if we are I don't think it's entirely mine," I replied, and immediately regretted it. Bill looked positively angry. I thought I'd better get back to the main point. "Surely there's no getting away from the fact that, if there is much healing it should be statistically observable. If it isn't observable then what reason have we got to assume its happening? I mean, plenty of people say they get healing with power crystals and things, but it's statistics that say if they do… right?"

Bill seemed unwilling to continue. "Looks like a subject for a PhD thesis," said Sandy brightly.

"I'm guessing someone's already studied this though," I replied, but Sandy didn't seem to be listening. Instead she was still musing out loud: "It's an interesting question – are Christians healthier?" We had just heard a talk all about the healing power of prayer, the content of which she had presumably discussed and helped to promote many times, and yet this question had apparently never occurred to her before.

Dr Phillip spoke for a while about how he felt it was necessary to keep one's faith out of one's job as a doctor, and the conversation moved to those who were not healed in spite of faith and prayer. Bill mentioned the previous vicar's wife, who died of bone cancer at a young age, "and she had all these people praying for her".

Pete had remained silent through all this, but now spoke up, "Isn't the point that we're healed in the next life? Isn't that what matters?" The entire point of the day's lecture had been that healing occurred in this world. Pete was again suggesting something directly at odds with Alpha doctrine.

"I see what you're saying," I replied. "But we've heard about all the positive effects here in this world. We can't talk about all the positive effects of God in this world, and ignore it when something goes wrong. He must be responsible for that too, surely?" Pete didn't answer. Meanwhile Bill seemed to be getting visibly angrier.

I decided to say nothing as we moved on to forgiveness, and the need for it to secure healing. "What I found really useful," said Bill "is the idea that you do have to forgive people but you don't have to trust them."

"Um, maybe I've been misinterpreting the Sermon on the Mount," I began, as Sandy giggled, "but I took it to mean you had to do more than forgive someone who'd wronged you – you had to encourage them to wrong you more. I'm thinking of where it says 'if he takes your cloak, give him your shirt as well'. And obviously 'turn the other cheek'."[9]

"What do you think it means?" came the classic Bill response.

"I don't know – am I misinterpreting it?" A period of silence followed.

"Do you think he was maybe using hyperbolic language, to say 'Don't worry about things in this world?'" asked Bill, in full Socratic mode. Where did turning the other cheek come into that, I wondered. He replied with an exposition of the Roman origins of the expression "go the extra mile". Turning the other cheek remained, as ever, a concept with unaddressed implications.

Bill soon took the opportunity to finish the discussion. Relations with him had soured. Sandy said goodbye in a jolly fashion: "Stuart's going to start his PhD project!" Bill said nothing at all. I had displeased The Leader.

Notes

1. Exodus 23:25-26: "Worship the Lord your God, and his blessing will be on your food and water. I will take away sickness from among you, and none will miscarry or be barren in your land, I will give you a full life span." Gumbel also says the "character of God" is a healing one based on Exodus 15:26: "...I will not bring on you any of the diseases I brought on the Egyptians, for I am the Lord, who heals you." The context here is a promise, if his people follow his commandments, not to inflict the same deadly plagues on Israel as were sent down upon Egypt.
2. 2 Kings 5.
3. See John 11:41-44.
4. See Acts 3 and 5:12-16. Interestingly, just prior to the latter passage, Acts 5:1-11 describes St Peter striking dead two wannabe disciples who'd failed to donate the entire proceeds of a land sale to the Christian church. While Biblical healing is taken as a precedent for today, death dealing isn't.
5. Matthew 28:16-20: "Then the eleven disciples went to Galilee, to the mountain where Jesus had told them to go. When they saw him, they worshipped him; but some doubted. Then Jesus came to them and said, 'All authority in heaven and on earth has been given to me. Therefore go and make disciples of all nations, baptising them in the name of the Father and of the Son and of the Holy Spirit, and teaching them to obey everything I have commanded you. And surely I am with you always, to the very end of the age.'"
6. Mark 16:17-18: "And these signs will accompany those who believe: In my name they will drive out demons; they will speak in new tongues; they will pick up snakes with their hands; and when they drink deadly poison, it will not hurt them at all; they will place their hands on sick people; and they will get well."
7. See chapter 7 for the closely related question of whether prayer works and the issue of confounding factors. As we discussed, the evidence is poor.
8. *A Life Worth Living*, p.13.
9. See e.g. Luke 6:29.

CHAPTER 15

Ordinary Christians Coming Together

The finale of the Alpha course wasn't really designed for the unconvinced. Titled "What About the Church?", it assumed that the previous weeks had persuaded the remaining attendees. Besides, it was hardly difficult to predict what a church-based group would say about the importance of church. An indicator was the recommended reading in the manual, confined to a book called *I Believe in the Church*. The only point of interest was how Bill would act after the previous week's contretemps.

I sat down at an empty table, soon to be joined by Anne and Sandy. Their main interest was Christmas preparations, particularly tablecloths. I sat in silence as they mutually empathized over present buying difficulties, until Sandy asked me about my own Christmas. She seemed surprised I was going abroad instead of enjoying a family gathering in Scotland. Nadine, who had arrived by this point, asked about the "blond one", meaning Malc, who had decided his soul was beyond saving by the Alpha course and had stayed at home. She giggled as she confided that she "always wanted to call me Graham". This seemed to be another manifestation of her impressionistic approach to reality, embodied more substantially in her attitude to religion. Fortunately the confessional merriment was redirected when Wilma appeared.

Eventually the conversation turned, via Wilma's happy experiences of household product testing – "You just go and have a chat about a product and they pay you", she said contentedly – to Hillsong and what the group might do after Alpha. Anne revealed that she'd "backslid" previously, ceasing her church attendance. As a result she had attended a Christian retreat where people shouted "amen" a lot, like Hillsong.

She didn't enjoy this. Emphasis on the battle against backsliding is a standard component of Evangelical Christianity. It looked as if a desire to avoid it happening again drove Anne's strenuous efforts to avoid the troublesome parts of the Bible and Alpha.

When we came to discuss Mike and Tom's sermons, Sandy commented surprisingly strongly that she found Mike "repetitive". I had often wondered what her position was. On the one hand she was the Deputy Leader, raised a Catholic; on the other she was scientifically trained, and seemed far more sceptical than Bill, who apparently wouldn't admit any faults at all in the Bible or the Alpha conception of Christianity. Every indicator was that he was a full blown fundamentalist, whereas she wasn't. She had even mocked American fundamentalists. Were their goals the same in promoting Alpha Christianity? She seemed uninterested in, perhaps even contemptuous of, the Charismatic Christianity that Alpha stemmed from and promoted. Yet it seemed she thought presenting a united front to the unbeliever was important, because she'd never directly disagreed with Bill in front of the group.

Anne and Sandy both seemed reasonable people, all in all. Neither came across as a fanatic or a zealot. Neither seemed to take demonic forces or homosexuality very seriously as a threat. And yet they were both actively working to promote a worldview that did. They seemed to believe that, however extreme the Alpha message might seem, it was worth pursuing because it brought people to God, and common sense would prevail in practice. In their case the latter seemed true, but what about Bill?

The talk began with thanks. Before launching into the jokes and heartfelt analogies, Mike wanted to "personally say a huge thank you to a huge team of people" – the caterers and other helpers. He joyfully announced bottles of wine for "helpers and leaders", and then presented bouquets to Liz and Alison, who had apparently prepared around 1200 meals in the name of God.

Mike's jokes had of course become a running joke. They had to continue though, even if in some post-ironic way. "Now, I normally start with a joke," said Mike, beaming at his audience. "My jokes are good aren't they?" he continued, to widespread guffawing. "I heard

Tom was starting a new church, and he, err, he was nervous about preaching. He was feeling a little dry, so he got a glass of water." Much spiel explained that he'd communicated his fears to various church staff – the warden, the verger, etc. – who all unilaterally decided to loosen his tongue with some gin in that water. To conclude this rehash of Gussie Fink-Nottle's prize-giving from *Right Ho, Jeeves*, the punch-line from the curate was: "It was a great sermon but there were a couple of things, Tim: there are TEN commandments, there are TWELVE disciples, and there are FOUR steps down the pulpit steps!"

Naturally enough, a prerequisite for promoting the shiny new Alpha path was to clear away fusty old images of churches. Mike declaimed the church's boring past, with its "enforced silence" and "excruciating boredom", through which the churchgoers had to "grit their teeth". "I passionately believe," Mike told us, "the church should be dynamic, not dry and dull." As my eyes wandered during this predictable message, I saw two female students vigorously hugging.

"But what is a church? It is emphatically NOT a building… although here we have a wonderful building." The Alpha concept of the Church was illustrated by several metaphors. Firstly, the Church is a manifestation of the "people of God". In the manual Gumbel delivers the usual Greek lesson: the New Testament word "ekklesia", from which the English term "ecclesiastical" derives, meant an assembly or gathering of people. According to Mark, if these people "profess the name of Jesus Christ" they are of the church.

The manual states that there is a "universal church" of 1,900 million Christians, composed of the "persecuted church", the "third world" church, and the "free world" church. This number includes Orthodox, Roman Catholic and Protestant Christians. Quite what it means to be part of this "universal church" is unclear. It certainly does not mean that members agree on fundamental issues. They use different Bibles, revere different saints, practise different rituals, and disagree wholesale on doctrine. To take a small sampling, many liberal Protestants do not agree with Gumbel's claims about the historical Jesus, his views on sex before marriage or homosexuality; Orthodox Christians are against statues of Jesus; Catholics are against priests marrying; the Free Presbyterian Church of Ulster is against almost everything, but particularly "Hell inspired" glossolalia as practised by Alpha.[1]

The way Gumbel presents his brand of Charismatic Christianity as uncontroversial and ecumenical warrants further investigation. Mike said division within the church was "ridiculous", but appeals for unity have been issued repeatedly during two thousand years of schism, excommunication and mutual persecution. The question isn't whether accord is desirable, but of actually reaching it among numerous factions whose differing interpretations are a testament to biblical ambiguity. As usual, Alpha glibly skates over serious issues, as if all disagreement were the result of an easily cleared-up misunderstanding. What meaning does the concept of a "Universal Church" have? Exactly how far do smiling Alpha proponents actually stretch their definition of "Christian"?

The various doctrinal differences have been, and in some cases are, enough for the various factions to deny that their opponents are Christian at all. During the Great Schism the Orthodox and Roman Catholic churches excommunicated one another. Beginning with Martin Luther in the early sixteenth century there have been Protestants who hold that, rather than being a fellow Christian, the Pope is the Antichrist – a view perhaps most famously reiterated in recent times by Ian Paisley, in the European Parliament in 1988.

While Gumbel and Mike allege to be ecumenical in their outlook, others are unapologetically not so, even just within Protestantism. In the last few centuries various factions, including Lutherans, Reformed Protestants, Mennonites, Anabaptists and Quakers have all been burned for heresy by other Protestants. Even today there are bitter Protestant divisions. Within Gumbel and Mike's own Anglican denomination there are rancorous divisions over homosexual priests.

Mike concluded his "people of God" speech with regrets about the decline of some Western churches, combined with hope for the rise of Evangelical Christianity. He was shocked that unlike the good old days "missionaries are coming here today!" Regrettably, "we've all seen churches close". It wasn't all bad, though, on account of the "spring harvest" and "new wine" coming in the form of a wave of Evangelicals that "really is very inspirational". While traditional churches were closing, with their "dry and dull" services, Mike saw progress in the rise of noisy, enthusiastic and "dynamic" Evangelical churches which will be much more effective at spreading the Lord's message, with their cell groups and "gifts of the spirit".

The second Alpha metaphor for the church was "the family of God". "You might not like me," joshed Mike, eyes a-twinkle, "but I'm your brother in Christ." Various Bible quotations bolstering this picture were produced, including 1 John 4:19-5:1, which says, among other things, "If anyone says, 'I love God,' yet hates his brother, he is a liar. For anyone who does not love his brother, whom he has seen, cannot love God, whom he has not seen". This citing of family connections was apparently intended to promote inter-denominational togetherness of the type that has so far eluded Christianity. "There are actually," Mike conceded, "huge debates in the Church of England, but there is still unity in the Church of England".

Was Alpha really helping, though? Sandy Millar, Anglican vicar of Holy Trinity Brompton before Nicky Gumbel, and originator of the Alpha Course, was reported shortly before this sermon as having been appointed as a Ugandan Bishop. Described by the vicar of Putney as one of many "[b]ridgeheads for the assault on the Church of England" in an article that urged Anglicans to rebuff "this mad bad clique with a bullying version of the Bible",[2] this move was connected with anti-homosexual hardliners who were threatening to withdraw from the Anglican Communion. Before this, in a sermon at HTB, Millar described the bid to allow gay clergy as, "a new demonic ideology that is attacking the very fabric of the church".[3] Mike said, "I love working with other denominations. I don't care about denominations." But Christians who buy the complete Alpha message – including Millar – assuredly do.

The alleged unity of Christianity was, Mike claimed, its main attraction in the early days. It "admitted slaves and women and treated them as equals". He singled out Paul, who was "actually a revolutionary because he said women were equal". The evidence for the early church as a force for revolutionary emancipation is not obvious, in spite of common Christian claims like this. Paul's epistles are quite clear in their anti-women, pro-slavery stance.

Nor was the church free of division in Paul's time. 1 Corinthians, for instance, contains a lengthy entreaty for unity in Corinth. And these were major doctrinal differences. As noted in chapter 6, crucial among them was the significance after Jesus of the Mosaic Law, including circumcision. Galatians is largely a tirade on this subject, clearly aimed at others who disagreed with Paul. While the coverage of this dispute in Acts 15 suggests Paul and Barnabas reached amicable agreement with Peter and James, there is reason to believe the seriousness of the dispute was airbrushed from the biblical picture. For instance, we know almost nothing about James, who was held to be the brother of Jesus and the leader of the Jerusalem church – too important a position for the minimal mention of him. The indications are that Paul won the factional dispute, and as a consequence we see little of his opponents' views except in the epistle of James (although it probably wasn't written by James), which is viewed by some as mocking Paul's doctrine of salvation.[4]

Given all this, Gumbel's urgings of "fellowship" and "forgiveness" between all Christians seem extraordinarily optimistic. Such a coming together would be unique in Christian history. But the call also seems dishonest, given the selectively literalist brand of Christianity actually promoted by Alpha – one that is inherently more hard-line and doctrinaire than the liberal variety, as well as far more preoccupied with supernatural phenomena and sexual morality. To the extent that Alpha goers read and believe the books and pamphlets – an activity in which we were repeatedly encouraged – they are likely to adopt a narrow fundamentalist conception of Christianity. Given the current splits just within Anglicanism this cannot be a recipe for unity, and Gumbel surely knows it.

In practical terms, in spite of Mike's vision of "ordinary Christians coming together", most Christians' understanding of church is surely their local congregation. The third metaphor, "The Body of Christ" seemed to assume this. Mike promoted the idea of "mutual dependence": "If someone's on the margins of the church, and seems to be drifting away, the church needs to follow them." "Diversity" was another theme, although its relevance seemed limited to distribution of catering, music and other duties between variously talented congregationists. "You already know my weaknesses!" joked Mike.

The final two conceptions of the church were vaguer still: "A Holy Temple" and "The Bride of Christ". The latter further illustrated biblical attitudes to marriage. "The chief end of man," Mike joyfully told us, "is to glorify God, to enjoy him. I find communion very moving. I'm a big softy." The girls nearby giggled. "A couple of times

I've been very close to tears". He paused, and gazed at the ceiling. "Such a huge privilege…"

Strangely, he ended with a call that seemed to undercut his earlier bridge building message. "We must witness to our parish. We cannot and must not change our doctrine and message to suit passing fashion. We love the Lord as a bride loves a bridegroom… a church should be a picture of heaven." After one final reminder about the bookstall we were off to our groups.

Given the hazy nature of the talk it wasn't surprising that the discussion was limited. Bill, slumped back in his chair, asked the usual questions about how we all found it. Wilma was non-committal: "It was good… yeah… nothing controversial. Quite a good talk."

"Why are you all dressed up then?" asked Anne. Bill was wearing a suit.

"Oh, I came straight from work – these are just my work clothes."

"I thought you were teaching?"

"I do some marking."

"What sort of marking?"

"Oh, just some masters stuff…"

"JUST some Masters stuff!" exclaimed Anne, agog like a teenager at a *Smash Hits* concert. Bill smiled.

With apparently nothing on the subject of the sermon worth raising Bill switched to the after-Alpha groups. The only one he knew anything about was Celia's. She wanted to start meeting straightaway to avoid "losing momentum". "I have to say I think that's nuts," said Bill. He thought people needed to recover, and that they wouldn't have time with Christmas preparations. This was the perfect cue for further musings about Christmas from Wilma and Nadine.

After a quarter an hour of festive gossip, I felt entitled to try to raise a couple of points – I was bored. "I had a question about the sermon. It's sort of been raised before… about unity – I was thinking, isn't that easier said than done?"

"What do you mean by that?" asked Bill, leaning back further into his slouch.

"Well, I asked about this before, but I didn't quite resolve it. It's sort of related. What about the different Bibles Christians use? I mean, we're all part of the same church but we use different Bibles?"

"Go on…" said Bill, approaching horizontal.

"Well, as an example, I'm thinking of those books missing from Protestant Bibles, like Maccabees."[5]

"Ah, those books were always questioned", said Bill, jumping forward.

"But they were in the Septuagint and the Vulgate,[6] and in everybody's Bibles until the sixteenth century when they got taken out."

"No, they were never really accepted."

"But they were there before Jesus, and after him, and just taken out of the Jewish canon after most of the Gospels were written."

"They were questionable before Jesus, and then there was a council that decided not to include them."

"OK. Well I just thought, since Christians had accepted them since before Jesus, the Catholics might have a reasonable case."

"No," was Bill's final pronouncement.

During all this exchange, Wilma had altered from being initially glassy eyed, to pulling faces at Nadine, to actually starting a separate conversation with her. She seemed very unhappy about the intrusion into her comfortable chatting space. I gave up on the Bible canon, and let her new conversation die out.

Since nobody said anything I ploughed on. "OK, leaving the Bible aside – I just wanted to get your view on that because last time I raised it you weren't here – I was wondering about different Christian beliefs. I mean, how do you define 'Christian'?"

"Someone who professes the name of Christ", replied Bill promptly.

"So what does that mean?"

"They hold Jesus to be the Son of God."

"So… what about Mormons, are they Christian?"

Bill pointed to Mormon's use of additional religious texts apart from the Bible. He seemed to think using Joseph Smith's revelations disqualified Mormons from the "universal church", even if it had no relation to the entry requirement he'd just stated.

"OK, how about Jehovah's Witnesses?"

"They don't believe Jesus was the Son of God." In fact they do believe this, albeit in a different sense.

"Oh OK, I thought they did from what they said… I've always

wondered about Christian Scientists too. I wonder what they get up to in those 'reading rooms'."

"I've always wondered that too!" said Sandy.

"I don't think they do either," said Bill. They do, again with a different notion of what this entails. *Science and Health with Key to the Scriptures*, their standard text, says that "Jesus Christ is not God, as Jesus himself declared, but is the Son of God".

"So, OK, they're kind of on the fringe, but what about, say, the Orthodox Christians?"

"They profess the name of Jesus."

"But they don't follow the same creed, right?"

"Yes, they do."

"But I thought the whole dispute was about the "filioque clause" in the Nicene Creed? I thought that was about not using the same creed".[7]

"YOU'RE not doing a masters are YOU?" snapped Wilma.

"I just looked at a few books," I replied, apologetically, but she was turning away, rummaging in her bag on the floor.

"The filioque clause… was a difference…" Bill began, looking round. He didn't seem so certain any more, but nobody was paying much attention. Wilma announced that she had to leave immediately, and bustled out, as Bill began to give a vague background, mentioning the Council of Nicea, and calling the disagreement "technical". This seemed fair, but it didn't remove the fact that it had contributed to arguably the biggest Christian division in history. "They still profess the name of Christ."

"So all anybody needs to do is believe Jesus is the Son of God, and they're a Christian? And it doesn't matter about what they think of the Trinity or whatever?"

"Yes," said Bill. Of course, this meant he'd been wrong about the Jehovah's Witnesses and Christian Scientists, but I wasn't sure of this at the time. In any case, there didn't seem much point in pursuing the matter further. After ten weeks of talks and discussion on "basic Christianity" we couldn't even pin down a consistent definition of what a Christian was.

We sat in silence for a moment, and then after looking at his watch Bill suggested we finish.

Notes

1. The Free Presbyterian Church of Ulster (Ian Paisley's church), takes an unforgiving view of Alpha. Its Rev. Paul Fitton authored an in-depth pamphlet on the subject, titled "The Alpha Course. Is it Bible-Based or Hell-Inspired?" He settled on the latter.
2. Giles Fraser, *Guardian*, 19th November 2005.
3. Bates, S. (2004). *A Church At War: Anglicans and Homosexuality*. I.B.Tauris, London, p.29.
4. For its opposition to Paul's doctrine of salvation through grace it was famously described by Luther, who inclined to Paul's radically pessimistic view of human redemption, as "this straw epistle".
5. 1 and 2 Maccabees are present in the Catholic and Orthodox Old Testament but are not considered scripture by most Protestants.
6. The Septuagint is the oldest Greek version of the Old Testament translated from Hebrew between the 3rd and 1st centuries BC. The Vulgate is the Latin version of the Bible prepared by Saint Jerome at the end of the 4th century CE and the authorised version of the Catholic Church.
7. The filioque clause is a disputed clause added to the Nicene Creed in 589, centred on the relative divinity of God and Jesus. Where the original Nicene Creed reads "We believe in the Holy Spirit... who proceeds from the Father", the amended, Roman Catholic version reads "We believe in the Holy Spirit... who proceeds from the Father and the Son" ("filioque" is Latin for "and the son"). The addition is accepted by the Roman Catholic Church but rejected by the Eastern Orthodox Church. This was at least the purported theological reason for the Great Schism that still separates Western and Eastern churches.

CHAPTER 16

Is There More to Alpha Than This?

So where did our Alpha "journey" lead? Plainly neither of us was convinced by Alpha's arguments. In fact, in our view the promotion of Alpha as a "rational" form of Christianity based on "firm historical evidence" is deeply misleading. Time and again, we were presented with inconsistent, evasive argumentation founded on, at best, an incomplete portrayal of evidence. Every description we heard of conversion or reassured faith hinged instead on emotional encounters, and it is hard to avoid concluding that Alpha's bid to appear reasoned and rigorous is little more than a public relations exercise.

Not that this bothers the audience. It didn't matter which area of Christian belief was under challenge; it didn't matter what defence Gumbel had produced; nobody we met had any doubt that Christian belief, however hazy in outline, was the right basic belief. All those irritating objections were no more than obstacles on a predefined course to God, to be hurdled via flawed argumentation or a "leap of faith" according to taste. The content of Gumbel's historical arguments appeared to be of almost no interest to our group. Biblical truth, if not always in an entirely literal sense, was taken as a given.

The beliefs built on this foundation varied according to background. Sandy, the deputy leader, did not suggest the Bible was infallible, and made clear some tolerance of homosexuality. She was not interested in the Hillsong brand of Christianity. Bill, by contrast, never accepted biblical fallibility, talked of exorcisms among other supernatural happenings, and ended up an enthusiastic Hillsong participant. The less committed members of our group seemed to have little firm idea what Christianity entailed.

This variability in audience reaction is not an outcome of Alpha's open-minded approach. To the extent that they disagreed, Bill was following Alpha's tenets and Sandy was not – on this, the course texts are quite clear. Nor was any doctrinal disagreement between them aired for the benefit of inquiring minds. Indeed, at no point did we hear any explicit disagreement between Christians at Alpha. Their personal views on, say homosexuality, were clearly subordinate to the overriding imperative of leading us to Jesus.

No blanket statement can be made, then, about the effect of Alpha. With stable Christians from a moderate background – Sandy was an example – Alpha's fundamentalist message does not seem to lead to even more extreme churches or beliefs. Given Alpha's connection with Anglicanism, many of those involved will inevitably fall into this category.

But Alpha straddles moderate Anglicanism and extremist fundamentalism, and the respectable people who staff its stalls and make friends with new "seekers" provide useful cover. With people like Sandy and Anne around it is far easier to imagine that Alpha doctrine is unremarkable, particularly when argument is discouraged and the more controversial edicts are saved for follow up texts. And yet the faith these people help promote is one founded on bizarre pseudo-historical argument and biblical literalism. It is one that promotes glossolalia and belief in demons and prayer healing, teaches that religious doubt originates from Satan, and views homosexuality as an illness. To the extent that any ideology is transmitted by the Alpha course, this is it.

We did not see anybody obviously converted to Alpha ideology – everybody we met holding those hardline views had already been convinced. But what we know of Bill's "journey" is perhaps instructive. When I first met Bill, the image was of a typical earnest liberal Christian, albeit one convinced that he had experienced multiple powerful supernatural phenomena. After attending Hillsong he became a regular there, and soon even gave up attending his beloved HTB. We continued to debate Christianity with Bill by email intermittently for several months after the course, and even met for a drink, but soon after enrolling in Hillsong's management course he broke off contact.

Hillsong has suffered from various scandals, notably the exposure of leader Brian Houston's father as a paedophile[1] and the false claims of "porn addict" pastor Michael Guglielmucci that he had terminal cancer.[2] There have also been accusations that Hillsong lacks accountability and is intolerant of dissent. When one follower wrote about these issues she was ejected from the church for "disrupting" services.[3]

But even an examination of Hillsong's openly espoused doctrine is disturbing to those outside hardcore Evangelical Christianity. It is noticeably more extreme and more political than anything in the Alpha course texts: wives are explicitly subordinate to husbands; abortion is evil; life did not arise via Darwinian evolution; the "end times" are imminent; and so on. Yet Bill was entirely unconcerned. Why would anybody from Alpha be, providing they bought its central message? Alpha teaches that the Bible is a manual for life. It teaches Christians to speak in tongues. It warns of demons. Yes, Hillsong is apparently more controlling and mercenary, and it takes biblical literalism further, but with its crowds of Spirit-inspired amen-shouters what could Hillsong be except God's work?

This illustrates what we believe is Alpha's main function. It rarely convinces atheists or non-Christians, as evidenced by our group and the statistics.[4] Rather, it acts as a conveyor belt to more hard-line Christianity for the suggestible. Almost nobody starts an Alpha Course an atheist and emerges a Christian; nearly everybody starts as a Christian of one type and, if the course has any effect, emerges a Christian of a different type, often convinced they weren't previously Christian at all. This is not to say that Alpha doesn't seek to convert atheists, just that Alpha more usually acts as a mechanism for converting liberal or nominal Christians into zealous Evangelicals. The churches filling up with those blessed by the Spirit are taking congregationists from more traditional Anglican and other churches.

Alpha is therefore contributing to the shift towards a more fundamentalist Christianity. If any result can be predicted from the current trends, it's towards a more polarised religious makeup to Britain – the evaporation of traditional Anglican woolliness, a reaction against tolerance for gay people and women priests, and a slant towards belief in speaking in tongues, demonic forces, and other supernatural phenomena. There are signs that this change will be accompanied by increasing political engagement by those holding these fundamentalist beliefs.

Once the course had finished we visited the Alpha epicentre, Holy Trinity Brompton, to witness Gumbel himself conduct an "informal" service. In appearance HTB was much like our local church, except it was located in Knightsbridge, so almost every congregationist appeared to drive a BMW or Mercedes. Then there was the enormous bookstore in the basement, carrying every conceivable Christian apologetic as well as collections of Alpha Videos (£139.99 for the set) in numerous languages. Naturally, all apologetical purchasing was accompanied by Christian soft rock, available in the expansive music section of the store.

The worship, too, was primarily about God rock. Each part of the service – the warm-up act, the praying, the sermon from Gumbel – was mingled with helpings of guitar-backed mantras. Unlike Hillsong, nobody felt moved to scream "Amen!" during the homily, but the music did provoke a great deal of hands-raised swaying. Many of the congregation seemed to achieve their "spiritual top-up" (to use Bill's words) primarily by standing, eyes closed, as waves of soothing musical platitudes washed over them. Watching the blissful young people, and one woman breaking out into some kind of improvisational dance routine, it seemed quite clear they weren't there to think: they were there to feel.

The sermon, and the experience of HTB as a whole, seemed to sum up the Alpha Course: intellectually empty and ultimately emotion-based. Any argument was pursued just as far as was required to reassure people who were more interested in feeling right than being right. This made no difference at all to people who wanted to feel the Holy Spirit through the medium of lighter-in-the-air musical experiences: they just needed a comforting voice. And all this is clearly working, as evidenced by the "Alpha International Campus" publicized when we were there – HTB is no longer big enough to contain Alpha.

Perhaps Alpha really does help people come to terms with life, but as far as we could determine it is only by providing a placebo belief system. It has no coherent content, but all the appearance of a carefully thought out logical scheme. It combines the hazy terminology of a liberal Anglican vicar with the certainty, and many of the beliefs, of an unreconstructed fundamentalist. The impression is of a fire and brimstone preacher who's taken PR advice.

The results, as we've noted, are variable. Alpha might just provide a happy place to sway and chant. Or it might provide the firm conviction that demons are hammering at the doors. Either way, it is one of the least honest forms of Christianity. It relies on the ignorance of its audience to shunt aside swathes of modern thought in a way that even 19th century liberal theologians felt unable to do, yet it trades off an Anglican reputation for openness and rational thought and moderation. It makes a grand pretence of logical examination of evidence, but then points to emotionalism and speaking in tongues to justify belief. It uses the Bible to promote socially conservative views, yet ignores that book's indefensible obscenities as well as Jesus's pacifism and preaching against personal wealth. Apparently the collapse in UK church attendance has led to this – only Alpha can stem the flow. But if the only way Christianity can now be promoted is via distortion of truth and feeling-based sing-a-long sessions, then surely it's time to give up the effort.

Notes

1. "The Lord's Profits". *Sydney Morning Herald*, 30th January 2003.
2. "Confessions of a porn addict pastor". *Daily Telegraph*, 29th August 2008.
3. Levin, T. (2007). *People in Glass Houses: An insider's story of a life in and out of Hillsong.* Black Inc, Melbourne.
4. Hunt, S. (2001) *Anyone for Alpha?* Darton, Longman and Todd Ltd.

Epilogue

The Hotel Kennedy, Fiji

I was in the cell that was my room at the Hotel Kennedy – Fiji's detention centre for unwanted foreign visitors. I was imprisoned and despairing, with no one in the outside world aware of my plight. My mental strength was at its lowest ebb with nothing to raise my spirits… or was there? I picked up the Bible and flicked through the thin pages. Of course! Here was a wise and ancient book, the contents of which had inspired millions down the ages — the divine word of our heavenly father! Here was someone I could turn to, someone who would listen to my prayers and rescue me from my plight.

The familiar titles rolled past on the pages – Genesis, Leviticus, Job (what a guy!), Mark, John, Corinthians – a wealth of inspiring stories of strength in the face of adversity followed by divine rewards. It all seemed obvious now and the book suddenly so attractive. This would be the moment of my conversion! Then my mind was flooded with memories of the Alpha course. First I had visions of the food. In my underfed state even the main courses were remembered as the most exquisite cuisine. Ah, and the cakes – the cakes always were very good at Alpha. And then all those friendly Christians: jolly, happy friendly faces striving to save my soul. I suddenly understood Alpha's popularity in prisons.

Then I put aside my isolation and hunger and remembered the message: the vapid, flimsy arguments, the web of contradictions, the tongues, the poor evidence, and the endless excruciating guitar bands. I looked at the Bible again and threw it back into the corner, embarrassed that I had almost been fooled. Why would I want to put my faith in that God? There was only one entity that could be trusted in this situation and I immediately started formulating an escape plan. The guards often left me when eating lunch downstairs. In typical South Pacific style the Hotel's security measures meant no fence and an open gate. I put on my trainers so I could run faster, fully intending to make a run for the main road, jump into a taxi and scream "take me to the embassy!", then doing another runner from the taxi once we got there, flinging open the embassy doors and bellowing for diplomatic immunity on UK soil.

As it happened this was unnecessary. I let my plan slip to a fellow inmate from Kiribati, who had recently arrived (the lack of power meant we shared many romantic candlelit dinners together in the evenings). He warned me that such an escape attempt, if it failed, could mean confinement in a proper criminal prison. Besides, what if I couldn't find a taxi? Heeding his words, I decided put my heroic plan on the backburner indefinitely.

A couple of days later I was awoken early in the morning and taken to the airport for deportation back to Vanuatu, only to find the airline had "forgotten" to book the ticket and the plane was now full. Fortunately, this provided me with the opportunity to explain the situation to the first reasonable immigration officer I'd met. She allowed me to purchase a ticket to Australia and I was duly dumped back at the airport the next day in my now soiled clothes.

It was an emotional journey on the plane back to Australia. In the turmoil of conflicting emotions – utter frustration, unfettered relief, raging anger and pure unadulterated happiness – I ended up embarrassing myself by becoming uncontrollably emotional while watching a contrived and trashy romantic comedy. But at least the Holy Spirit had not come upon me.

APPENDIX A

Drowning in Evidence

In his Alpha Bible reading course book, *30 Days*, Gumbel states:

"It is not belief in Jesus that is irrational but unbelief. It is irrational not to believe in the face of overwhelming evidence."

"You could thank God that he has not left us without evidence and that our faith is based on good historical grounds."[1]

According to Tom we are "drowning in evidence" for Jesus. In the main course text Gumbel assures his readers that a Christian's "leap of faith" is "based on firm historical evidence". There is, he says, "a great deal of evidence for Jesus' existence".[2]

Leaving aside the spurious manuscript-counting argument described in Chapter 3, the sole non-biblical support offered for these claims was a reference to Josephus, Tacitus and Suetonius.

These sources are not impressive, as explained below. But it should be borne in mind that this old debate risks obscuring a more important issue. These sources could not verify the contents of the Gospels even if they were independent, uncorrupted and unambiguous. On earthly matters they lack content: they tell us almost nothing about Jesus's life. On the supernatural, they lack authority, because the direct say-so of an ancient historian is not enough to credit divine status, or we would have thousands of gods. What this discussion does provide is a good illustration of the gap between reality and Gumbel's blithe claims.

Josephus

Josephus's main reference to Jesus, often called *Testimonium Flavianum*, is quoted in Gumbel's book with an endnote admitting that "some suggest… the text has been corrupted":

"Now there was about this time, Jesus, a wise man, if it be lawful to call him a man, for he was a doer of wonderful works – a teacher of such men as receive the truth with pleasure. He drew over to him both many of the Jews, and many of the Gentiles. He was [the] Christ; and when Pilate, at the suggestion of the principal men amongst us, had condemned him to the cross, those that loved him at first did not forsake him, for he appeared to them alive again the third day, as the divine prophets had foretold these and ten thousand other wonderful things concerning him; and the tribe of Christians so named after him, are not extinct at this day."[3]

The other Josephus passage that mentions Jesus (which Gumbel doesn't cite) does so obliquely, when recounting his brother James's death at the hands of the Jewish High Priest.[4]

No serious scholar believes the Gumbel *Testimonium* is genuine. Most importantly, Josephus was an observant Jew, yet it refers to Jesus in extravagant, Christian terms as the foretold Messiah resurrected. Josephus did not discount the idea of Jewish prophecy being fulfilled in his time. He felt the Emperor Vespasian was an agent of God, sent to punish the Jews in fulfilment of Numbers 24.17-19.[5] Such instruments of divine vengeance were in the Old Testament tradition of Egyptian and Babylonian kings. The problem is that Gumbel's *Testimonium* is in a quite different, identifiably Christian, tradition, specifically incorporating Gentiles and Gospel resurrection elements.

There is no doubt that Josephus did not share this tradition. He wrote a Jewish apologetic called *Against Apion*. He fought the Romans at the head of a Jewish army at a time when Christianity was dissociating itself from Judaism. On top of this, Origen, the third century church father, referred to the second reference to Jesus in Josephus's work, and to John the Baptist[6] (specifically to prove his existence), but not the

167

Testimonium. Indeed he explicitly contradicts it by saying Josephus did not believe in Jesus as the Messiah. For these reasons and others, the scholarly consensus is that the *Testimonium* is an original passage mentioning Jesus altered to incorporate a pro-Christian message by later apologists. For instance Geza Vermes, the doyen of historical Jesus scholars, states that the passage "certainly contains elements which cannot be authentic (for example, 'if indeed one might call him a man'; 'he was the Messiah', and a reference to the resurrection)."[7] E.P.Sanders, another respected historian, puts it more strongly:

"The Jewish historian [Josephus] certainly knew something about Jesus, and there is a paragraph on him in the *Antiquities* (18.63f). But Josephus' works were preserved by Christian scribes, who could not resist the temptation to revise the text and thus make Josephus proclaim that Jesus 'was the Messiah'; that he taught 'the truth'; and that after his death he was 'restored to life'. Failing a fluke discovery, we shall never know what Josephus actually wrote."[8]

That Gumbel acknowledges this problem only in a mealy-mouthed and misleading way does not reflect well on him. It is hard to escape the conclusion that he is relying on audience credulity rather than evidence to burnish Jesus's messianic credentials.

Josephus probably did mention the biblical Jesus (alongside, as it happens, a dozen other men named Jesus) but at most he revealed that he was crucified and was the brother of James. This point does not hinge on the forged *Testimonium* elements being discounted. Even if we accept them, they provide no biographical information – just a bald assertion that he was the resurrected Messiah (and we do not take the title of Suetonius's biography of Julius Caesar, "the Deified Julius", to mean that Julius Caesar was a god). In this sense it does not matter that Gumbel's quotation is forged because his argument is discredited by a more fundamental flaw.

Note also that Josephus's coverage of Jesus stands in contrast to that of other miracle workers and prophets, such as John the Baptist, about whom he supplies far more detail (detail which, in fact, contradicts the Gospels[9]). John the Baptist was, if Josephus's coverage is any guide, more significant at the time, as was another mysterious prophet referred to as "the Egyptian".[10] Given this, it is perhaps not surprising that Christian forgers actively sought to bolster Jesus's messianic claims. But why was the real evidence so weak that it provoked this fraud?

Tacitus

Tacitus refers to Nero scapegoating Christians:[11]

"Nero fastened the guilt and inflicted the most exquisite tortures on a class hated for their abominations, called Christians by the populace. Christus, from whom the name had its origin, suffered the extreme penalty during the reign of Tiberius at the hands of one of our procurators, Pontius Pilatus, and a most mischievous superstition, thus checked for the moment, again broke out not only in Judaea, the first source of the evil, but even in Rome, where all things hideous and shameful from every part of the world find their centre and become popular."

Note that they were a sect founded by "Christus" (a latinised form of the Greek Christos, meaning "anointed one") not "Jesus". If Tacitus had been working from Roman records he wouldn't have used the religious term "Christus" for Jesus, and he probably also wouldn't have given Pilate the anachronistic title "procuratorem".[12] This suggests that he was passing on general gossip. In any case he supplies less detail than Josephus: just that Jesus was killed by Pilate.

Suetonius

The sentence usually produced to show that Suetonius referred to Jesus reads:

"He [the Emperor Claudius] expelled from Rome Jews who were constantly making disturbances at the instigation of Chrestus".[13]

There has been some debate about what "Chrestus" means. Jesus never went to Rome, and was crucified well before Claudius became emperor in 41 CE, so any instigation would have been from beyond the grave. A common argument is that Chrestus was a garbled reference to Christian beliefs, rather than a person (Sanders holds this view; Vermes is more equivocal). However it is also possible that a troublemaker named Chrestus was at work in this time; we know from inscriptions that this was a common name.[14]

Later in the same work Suetonius writes, with respect to Nero:

"During his reign many abuses were severely punished and put down: ... punishment was inflicted on the Christians, a class of men given to a new and mischievous superstition..."[15]

He now has the vowel correct, and he refers to Christianity as a "new" superstition, rather than a sect of Judaism, both of which cut against the standard Christian line regarding Chrestus. This sentence is less popular with Christian apologists, although unlike the first it is at least definitely about Christians. In both cases Suetonius is at most referring to Christians, not Christ, and gives no biographical detail.

Extra-Biblical Sources in General

An overriding difficulty with both Tacitus and Suetonius is that they wrote long enough after Jesus's life – both around 110 CE – that their sources could not have been first hand witnesses. Their testimony therefore tells us nothing more than that there were Christians in the Roman world in 110 CE, and provides no independent confirmation of anything regarding Jesus. E.P.Sanders summarizes the problem:

"[K]nowledge of Jesus was limited to knowledge of Christianity; that is, had Jesus' adherents not started a movement that spread to Rome, Jesus would not have made it into Roman histories at all. The consequence is that we do not have what we would very much like, a comment from Tacitus or another Gentile writer that offers independent evidence about Jesus, his life and his death."

Nevertheless, Gumbel suggests that Suetonius and Tacitus show that Jesus-the-risen-Messiah existed.[16] They do not, any more than Pliny's *Natural History* shows Zoroaster, inventor of magic, existed.[17]

Taken together, all they tell us is that a religious leader was executed in Tiberius's reign. Even if Tacitus and Suetonius spoke of the biblical Jesus, they would still say nothing about biblical accuracy regarding the events of his life – events upon which the Christian faith is based.

Among these three sources presented by Alpha, the sole potential independent confirmation we have of anything in the Bible comes from Josephus, who informs us of nothing beyond Jesus's execution by Pilate. Even if, against the evidence, we buy the entire quotation in Gumbel's book, we don't know what Jesus said, where he went, or what miracles he performed: we must rely instead on the Gospels for this information.

These three authors are widely acknowledged to be the most persuasive non-biblical sources on Jesus, which is why Gumbel mentioned them and not others. The alternatives typically cited – Pliny the Younger, Philo, Thallus, the Talmud – are at least as inconclusive, either saying nothing detailed about Jesus himself, or being written too late to be independent of the Christian tradition, or both.

To reiterate, the sum total of independent knowledge we have from sources outside the Bible is that a religious troublemaker named Jesus or Christ was crucified by Pilate – far from a unique incident at that time.

Notes

1. 30 Days, p.17.
2. Questions of Life, p.21.
3. Josephus, *Jewish Antiquities*, 18.63, quoted in *Questions of Life*, p.22. Gumbel uses here the nineteenth century Whiston translation but the numbering system of the more modern Loeb translation.
4. Josephus, *Jewish Antiquities*, 20.200.
5. Josephus, *Jewish War*, 6.312-313.
6. His reference is to Josephus, *Jewish Antiquities*, 18.116. Josephus does not connect John the Baptist to Jesus, instead calling him a "good man" who "commanded the Jews to exercise virtue".
7. Vermes, G. (2005). *Who's Who in the Age of Jesus*. Penguin, p.163.
8. Sanders, E. P. (1995). *The Historical Figure of Jesus*. Penguin, p.50.
9. Josephus attributes John's execution to his potential to incite rebellion. This contradicts the Gospels, which put it down to the machinations of Herod Antipas's wife, Herodias, inspired by John's condemnation of their marriage (Mark 6:18-28, Matthew 14:3-11, Luke 3:19-20, Luke 9:9). An

additional clash lies in the date. Herod Antipas didn't marry Herodias until 34 CE, which is generally deemed to be after Jesus died, yet Luke is clear John died before Jesus (see Luke 9:9).

10. E.P.Sanders (op. cit., p.50-51) says that "if we measure the impact of prophetic figures by the degree of disturbance they caused, we shall conclude that Jesus was less important in the eyes of most of his contemporaries than were John the Baptist and the Egyptian."

11. Tacitus, *Annals*, 15.44.

12. That is, he refers to him as "procurator". His title at the time was "prefect", as we know from a contemporary inscription.

13. Suetonius, G. Tranquillus, *De Vita Caesarum*, Divi Claudi, 25.4.

14. For a brief discussion of "Chrestus", see *Who's Who in the Age of Jesus*, p.72.

15. Suetonius, G. Tranquillus, *De Vita Caesarum*, Nero, 16.2.

16. *Questions of Life*, p.21-22: "There is a great deal of evidence for Jesus' existence... For example, the Roman Historians Tacitus (directly) and Suetonius (indirectly) both write about him."

17. Pliny the Elder, in *Natural History* 30.2, says that Zoroaster, presumed founder of Zoroastrianism, invented magic. Elsewhere he reports the view that Zoroaster survived in the desert for thirty years on a type of anti-ageing cheese (*Natural History* 11.97).

APPENDIX B

Expressions of God's Love

There are a multitude of examples of God killing people in the Bible either directly or via his chosen people. Table 1 reports the 10 most devastating smitings.[1] Minor infractions have also brought divine wrath, often in bizarre form – the top 10 of God's pettiest killings are shown in Table 2.

Table 1: God's Greatest Hits

1.	The LORD struck down an army of 1 million Cushites in the Valley of Zephathah. The single most devastating smiting in the Bible.	2 Chronicles 14:9-14
2.	GOD routed the army of Israel and delivered them into the hands of the forces of Judea who then killed 500,000 Judeans.	2 Chronicles 13:15-17
3.	The angel of the LORD put to death 185,000 sleeping Assyrian men.	Isaiah 37:36
4.	When Gideon attacked the Midianite camp GOD made 120,000 Midianite swordsmen kill each other.	Judges 7:22, 8:10
5.	The Arameans thought the LORD was a God of the hills and not the valleys so he delivered the Aramean army to the Israelites who then killed 100,000 in one day.	1 Kings 20:28-29

6.	GOD ordered Moses to take vengeance on the Midianites. After killing all the men and burning and plundering all the Midianite towns Moses became angry because his commanders had not killed all the women. So they slaughtered all the women and boys except the female virgins. Approximately 90,000+ Midianites were massacred in total. After that the soldiers only had to stay outside the camp for 7 days to cleanse themselves before they were forgiven.	Numbers 31:1-35
7.	After the LORD incited David to take a census of the fighting men in Israel his response was to kill 70,000+ in a plague for taking the census.	2 Samuel 24:13-16, 1 Chronicles 21:7-15
8.	In Beth Shemesh 50,070 men were put to death by GOD for looking into the Ark of the LORD.	1 Samuel 6:19
9.	After defeat at the hands of the Israelites the remains of the Aramean army escaped to the city of Aphek only for 27,000 of them to be killed when GOD made a wall fall on top of them.	1 Kings 20:30
10.	"The LORD defeated Benjamin before Israel, and on that day the Israelites struck down 25 100 Benjamites". They then went to Gibeah and "put the whole city to the sword".	Judges 20:35-37

1. Note: God's killing is not yet over. According to Revelations if the end times were to come this year another 3.25 billion would be killed.

Table 2: God's Pettiest Hits

		Find it in:
1.	The Israelites complained about the poor quality of the food (there was no bread and water and the food was described as "miserable"). In response, several were killed when the LORD sent venomous snakes amongst them.	Numbers 21:4-6
2.	GOD put Onan to death for masturbating ("spilling his seed") instead of impregnating his sister-in-law.	Genesis 38:8-10
3.	GOD turned Lot's wife into a pillar of salt for looking behind her at the destruction of Sodom and Gomorrah.	Genesis 19:26
4.	GOD ordered Moses to stone to death a Man for gathering wood on the Sabbath.	Numbers 15:32-36
5.	GOD burned to death 250 men when they were offering incense.	Numbers 16:35
6.	A prophet was killed by a lion for believing another prophet's lie.	1 Kings 13:1-24
7.	Uzzah was struck down by GOD for stopping the Ark of the LORD from falling off a cart after the oxen stumbled.	2 Samuel 6:6-7, 1 Chronicles 13:9-10
8.	After Ahaziah fell through the lattice of his upper room he consulted the God of Ekron, Baal-Zebub, to see if he would recover so GOD killed him for talking to a different God.	2 Kings 1:2-17
9.	The LORD ordered 3,000 people to be killed for dancing around Aaron's golden calf. He then sent down a plague to finish the job.	Exodus 32:27-28, 35
10.	An officer guarding the gate disbelieved Elijah's message from the LORD that the price of 1kg of flour and 2kg of Barley would plummet to just one shekel the next day and so was trampled to death by a crowd of people.	2 Kings 7:17-20

APPENDIX C

A Manual for Life

Alpha promotes the Bible as an apparently infallible "manual for life". The Alpha lifestyle requires following this manual closely. This quiz will indicate if you are ready to do so.

1. You are a woman attending church. The sermon has raised some questions. What do you do?
    a. Ask your pastor to explain.
    b. Remain silent and ask your husband submissively at home.
    c. Consult the Bible yourself.

2. Your son interrupts you as you are trimming your beard while wearing your favourite polyester cotton socks. He refuses to leave you in peace so you stone him to death. What sin(s) did you commit?
    a. Stoning your son to death.
    b. Wearing mixed fibres.
    c. Trimming your beard.
    d. b and c.

3. You are a mother giving birth, and labour has become painful. Who is to blame?
    a. Your doctor.
    b. Your husband.
    c. You.

4. You are a Chosen man attacked by a rival tribe. Fortunately you slaughter all the men and acquire a captive woman. What do you do next?
    a. Shave her head.

b. Throw away her clothes.

c. Wait one month before impregnating her.

d. All of the above.

5. It's Sunday, and you spot a neighbour taking disadvantaged children on an outing to Legoland. You put him to death for breaking the Sabbath. A female police officer comes to arrest you. Do you:

   a. Go quietly with her to the police station.

   b. Apologize but explain that the Sabbath is Holy.

   c. Tell her to be silent and pronounce that as a woman she has no authority over you.

6. You are an older god-fearing man travelling on the bus to your weekly prayer group. A young woman offers you her seat and you accept. Suddenly you perceive the very real risk that she might have been menstruating. Should you:

   a. Forget about it and remain seated.

   b. Form an angry mob and arrange for her to be stoned to death outside the city gates.

   c. Wash your clothes, bathe in water and resign yourself to the fact that you are unclean until evening.

7. You are served a burnt beef burger at an Alpha supper. As an ethical consumer which one of the following should *not* concern you?

   a. Whether the burger was sacrificed to Baal

   b. Whether the cow was strangled.

   c. Whether the cow was slaughtered in a kosher fashion.

   d. Whether the cow was raised according to strict organic standards.

8. Your 11-year old daughter is spotted "knowing" an unknown male. Observers report that she did not cry out. Should you:

   a. Report the man to the police for paedophilia.

   b. Insist that the man pay you 50 shekels.

   c. Dispatch her to the city gates for a stoning.

9. You find yourself in financial difficulties. Undeterred, you head out to the streets to help the spiritually bankrupt via loud preaching. A mumbling vagrant's dog rubs against your leg and transfers an aggressive strain of scabies. What is your course of action?

   a. Leave it to fester. It was His will.

b. Make a doctor's appointment.
c. Wash your clothes, shave off all your hair, bathe in water, stay outside your house for 7 days and then shave all your hair again (including eyebrows). Then on the 8th day bring to your church 2 male lambs and a 1 year old ewe lamb (all without defects) with 11 ½ pints of fine flour/oil mix and ½ pint of oil. The Vicar will direct you from there.
d. Wash yourself as in c) but on the 8th day bring to the church 1 male lamb, 4 pints of fine flour/oil mix, ½ pint of oil, and 2 doves or young pigeons.

10. You spot a woman praying in Church, sporting a clearly visible and uncovered double plait hairstyle. Do you:
    a. Concentrate on your chinwag with God.
    b. Produce the portable electric shaver you carry for just such occasions and shave the woman's head.
    c. Politely tell the woman that the double plait takes the shine out of her hair and suggest she change it to a classic beehive, which would complement the triangular shape of her face and give her a great look all over.

11. Grasshoppers, houseflies, rabbits and young goats cooked in their mother's milk are all unclean foods: True / False

12. Five years ago you planted an apple tree in your garden. Four years ago you planted a pear tree. Three years ago you planted an orange tree. They are all bearing ripe fruit ready for eating. What should you do with each?
    a. Eat them all. They are God's gift.
    b. Eat the apples, offer praise to the Lord for the pears and leave the oranges.
    c. Eat the pears, leave the apples and offer praise to the Lord for the oranges.
    d. Eat the oranges, leave the pears and offer praise to the Lord for the apples.

Answers

1. b) 1 Corinthians 14:34-35: "[W]omen should remain silent in the churches. They are not allowed to speak, but must be in submission, as the Law says. If they want to inquire about something, they should ask their own husbands at home; for it is disgraceful for a woman to speak in the church." Ephesians 5:22-24: "Wives, submit to your husbands as to the Lord. For the husband is the head of the wife as Christ is the head of the church, his body, of which he is the Saviour. Now as the church submits to Christ, so also wives should submit to their husbands in everything."

2. d) Leviticus 19:27: "Do not cut the hair at the sides of your head or clip off the edges of your beard."; Leviticus 19:19: "Do not wear clothing woven of two kinds of material."; Deuteronomy 22:11: "Do not wear clothes of wool and linen woven together." According to Deuteronomy 21:18-21, rebellious sons should be taken to the city gates and stoned to death.

3. c) After Adam revealed that he had eaten the forbidden fruit given to him by Eve in the Garden of Eden God says in Genesis 3:16: "I will greatly increase your pains in childbearing; with pain you will give birth to children. Your desire will be for your husband, and he will rule over you."

4. d) Deuteronomy 21:10-14, titled "Marrying a Captive Woman" requires you to do all these things.

5. c) The Sabbath is indeed holy and you were right to put the man to death for taking the children out: Exodus 31:14: "Observe the Sabbath, because it is holy to you. Anyone who desecrates it must be put to death"; Numbers 15:32-36: "...a man was found gathering wood on the Sabbath day. Those who found him gathering wood brought him to Moses and Aaron and the whole assembly... Then the LORD said to Moses, 'The man must die. The whole assembly must stone him outside the camp.'". However, a woman has no authority over a man to arrest him: 1 Timothy 2:12: "I do not permit a woman to teach or to have authority over a man; she must be silent."

6. c) Leviticus 15:19-22: "When a woman has her regular flow of blood, the impurity of her monthly period will last seven days, and anyone who touches her will be unclean till evening... Whoever touches anything she sits on must wash his clothes and bathe with water, and he will be unclean till evening."

7. d) Food should be prepared in a strict manner as stated in Leviticus

17. Any dealings with other Gods, such as Baal, are forbidden in numerous passages such as 2 Kings 1:2-17 and Deuteronomy 13. In one version of Acts 15:20 Christians are instructed to abstain from food polluted by false idols, from animals killed by strangling, and from blood.

8. b) Deuteronomy 22:28-29: "If a man happens to meet a virgin who is not pledged to be married and rapes her and they are discovered, he shall pay the girl's father fifty shekels of silver. He must marry the girl, for he has violated her."

9. d) Leviticus 14 lays out what to do if you contract an infectious skin disease. If you are too poor to afford the full quota of goods, as in answer (c), you must present the modified quota laid out in Leviticus 14:21-22.

10. b) 1 Corinthians 11:5-6: "…every woman who prays or prophesies with her head uncovered dishonours her head… If a woman does not cover her head, she should have her hair cut off".

11. False. According to Leviticus 11:20-22 grasshoppers are clean foods suitable for eating whereas the others are unclean.

12. b) Leviticus 19:23-25: "When you enter the land and plant any kind of fruit tree, regard its fruit as forbidden. For three years you are to consider it forbidden; it must not be eaten. In the fourth year all its fruit will be holy, an offering of praise to the LORD. But in the fifth year you may eat its fruit."

APPENDIX D

Flushed them down the toilet

One of the most well known causes of mystical experiences is temporal lobe epilepsy. Patients with this condition sometimes have powerful religious experiences and it has been suggested that St Paul and other ancient religious leaders suffered from it. One famous case is that of Russian author Fyodor Dostoevsky.[1] Sometimes before suffering a seizure Dostoevsky would be gripped by an "ecstatic aura" and feel the powerful presence of God. He once described the experience to a friend saying "God exists, He exists... the air was vibrant and full of sound and I felt that heaven had come down to earth and had absorbed me. I really perceived God and was imbued with him." This casts an interesting light on Dostoevsky's morality-based arguments for religion.

Other temporal lobe epileptics are described in the medical literature as becoming devoutly religious.[2][3] Although a result of the epilepsy, these experiences and changes in religious behaviour do not necessarily occur at the same time as a seizure. One woman experienced at least five religious conversions over an 11-year period, describing one conversion as "like seeing God", developed a writing compulsion and became preoccupied with cosmic and global issues. She would repeatedly sketch a drawing of the site of one of her religious conversions and also developed a strong dislike for the sight of giraffes and polka dots of a particular size. Other patients have reported experiences including the feeling that they were "literally in heaven", having conversations with God, believing themselves to be the Son of God, and seeing visions of the crucifixion.

Other researchers have suggested that dysfunction in other areas of the brain can explain religious behaviours and experience.[456] Theories such as these highlight areas of the brain that are associated with mystical experience, although they are not well attested to at present.

Mystical experiences therefore can be the result of pathological brain processes but it isn't plausible as a general explanation. Epileptics such as Dostoevsky are rare, and some studies have found that less than 2% of temporal lobe epileptics have related religious experiences.[7]

Furthermore, clinicians have pointed out that mystical experiences in psychiatric patients with mental disorders are typically interpreted in a negative manner and usually produce extreme fear and sometimes violence in the sufferer. There is the case already mentioned of the man who severed his testicles and "flushed them down the toilet". Others have gouged out their own "sinful eyes" or attacked others, such as the Texan mother who drowned her five children in order to save their souls from Satan.[89] In comparison many people who claim to have had religious experiences do not seem to be dysfunctional at all, and Bill and the others seemed to relish and rejoice in their experiences. In fact, they often seemed to be a core basis of their faith, for which they were thankful to God. If the data does not fit perfectly to put all Christians under the "mad" umbrella of delusional psychotics, and they aren't lying, that leaves us with the claim that they are telling the truth. Is it really possible that these mystical experiences might in some way be "real"?

One recent theory is the neuropsychological model of Andrew Newberg and Eugene D'Aquili, which views mystical experiences as a naturally occurring phenomenon.[1011] Before going further we must stress that we are not claiming it is the definitive answer — criticisms of Newberg and D'Aquili and their responses can readily be found.[1213] [141516] There is also not enough space here to provide a full explanation of the theory. This would require detailed description of neurological phenomena, and can be found in the references given. The point here is to illustrate that there are reasonable modern explanations for mystical experiences that do not entail labelling the claimants as mad or lying.

The most relevant aspect of the theory for the Alpha course is the role of rituals in mystical experience. Newberg and D'Aquili posit that rhythmic stimulation and religious rituals activate important areas of the brain and nervous system and set in motion a neurological chain of events that "generate emotional discharges….and….result in unitary states that, in a religious context, are often experienced as some degree of spiritual transcendence". Their definition of a ritual is anything highly rhythmic, patterned and repetitious. Thus, rituals do not have to be religious and they include non-religious events such as political rallies, sporting events and music concerts. This is an important point.

What do they suggest happens during a religious ritual? Firstly, rituals and rhythmic stimulation induce different bodily states by altering the function of the nervous system.[17] Essentially, rituals serve to either relax or arouse an individual. "Slow" rituals (e.g. chanting, prayer, meditation, etc.) promote a state of relaxation (quiescence) whereas "rapid rituals" (e.g. dancing and singing) act to put the body in a state of arousal.[18] If pushed to extremes by ritual the body can enter into what is termed a state of "hyperarousal" or "hyperquiescence". Hyperarousal, a state of intense concentration and alertness, is often seen during activities such as piloting jet planes and racing cars. Individuals in this state often report feelings of "channelling great quantities of energy through their consciousness". Hyperquiescence is a state of extreme relaxation normally seen during sleep but accompanied by "heightened alertness and awareness".[19]

The next step involves how the parts of the nervous system responsible for producing these states are connected to and affect key brain areas involved in the perception of the self and the world. Most notably they affect the limbic system, which is associated with complex emotional expression and the generation of emotions and mood. By stimulating the limbic system via the nervous system rituals can produce two interesting effects.

The first is that neural input to selected areas of the brain can become inhibited in an effect known as deafferentation. Essentially, if the body is driven to extreme arousal or relaxation by ritual, the increase in neural activity activates the limbic system. One function of the limbic system is to regulate and promote equilibrium in the brain. Thus if neural activity reaches excessively high levels it will reduce or block neural flow to and from that brain area, forcing that area to work without the required input that it depends on to function normally. When this happens in religious rituals deafferentation occurs in an area responsible for creating a "three dimensional sense of the body" and for "orienting the body in space".[20] This area receives information from multiple senses, defines our sense of self and allows us to draw a distinction between our bodies and the rest of the universe. Once deafferentated, the brain is attempting to define the self without sufficient neural information from the senses. The result is that the brain cannot adequately recognize the boundaries of the self, which "blurs" with either a particular object of focus (such as a portrait of the Virgin Mary) or the world more generally. The individual experiences this as a unitary experience with feelings such as "spacelessness" and "timelessness".

The limbic system does not simply cut off a brain area like an on/off switch. Instead when deafferentation occurs neural input is gradually and progressively reduced. For this reason Newberg and D'Aquili posit a "continuum of unitary experience". At one end of the continuum is our everyday state of mind. Low levels of deafferentation may result in mild unitary experiences, such as feelings of unity with other members of a congregation at a Church service. Further deafferentation may result in more intense states, characterized by religious awe and rapture. Towards the far end of the continuum an individual may experience "trancelike states... featuring moments of ecstasy and hyperlucid visions". At the very end of the continuum lies what the authors describe as Absolute Unitary Being which would include the life-changing experiences as written about by Sister Margareta or the experience of the "void" by Buddhist monks.

The second potential effect of rhythmic rituals is the promotion of strong emotional states that occur concurrently with deafferentation. Rhythmic behaviours such as singing, dancing and chanting can produce intensely pleasurable feelings[21] and other aspects of ritual (such as burning fragrance) act to stimulate multiple senses at the same time. The effects of the sensory aspects of the ritual can also be augmented by religious cues and behaviours (e.g. the sign of the cross, kneeling for prayer, bows, handshakes) that can act as powerful conditioned cues for these feelings. An additional role of the limbic system is to look out for signs or danger and opportunity. If the limbic system is electrically stimulated for long enough in animals they respond with "fear, cringing and withdrawal". This fear response, when coupled with the blissful calm of a hyper quiescent state and deafferentation is experienced as religious awe, ecstasy or the presence of God.[22]

Here it is worth noting that other research has suggested that religious cues can also evoke "remembered emotions" that augment the mystical experience.[23] When past emotions are remembered they can be "refelt" in the present, and this can be triggered by environmental cues, just as an old song can remind you of how you felt at a particular time of your life. Furthermore, it is suggested that these "refelt" emotions can be developed and trained by the repetition of ritual so that they can be recalled more easily. Thus, a ritual may become more efficient at triggering a mystical experience over time.

It should be clear that several elements of a typical Evangelical service would, according to the theory, tend to induce mystical feelings in a hypothetical Christian participant. Repetitive and rhythmic music would stimulate their arousal system, driving it to higher levels of activation until the increased level of neural activity caused their limbic system to inhibit neural input to the orientation association area. The Christian would then undergo a blurring of their sense of self – absorption into the music and rapturous feelings of unity with other members of the congregation. The service would stimulate areas of the limbic system associated with pleasurable psychological states, triggering anything from mildly pleasant sensations to ecstasy. At the same time the prolonged sermonising and unusual behaviour of the preachers, not to mention people breaking into tongues and/or animal noises, would catch the attention of other parts of the limbic system eliciting a mild fear response. In addition, if our Christian had attended similar services many times in the past, the religious symbolism on the stage and the memory of the service could trigger "re-felt" emotions, adding to the experience. This combination of pleasant emotions, a mild fear response, and blurring of the edges of the self might be interpreted by our Christian as a feeling of religious awe and ecstasy, possibly even as a sense of God himself.

Newberg and D'Aquili stress that ritual alone cannot necessarily produce mystical experiences and that they are dependent on the context. If a ritual is to be completely successful in producing a religious experience the participant must have some kind of cognitive reason for engaging in the ritual. For example, meditators are much more successful in reaching altered mental states if they use mantras that have a personal meaning. So if a ritual has little deep meaning then it is less likely that it will produce any kind of religious feeling. This might help to explain why we failed to be moved by Alpha's guitar strumming-backed chants and sermons, whereas other members of the congregation were rapt.

As noted earlier, non-religious rituals can involve these same processes. The only difference is the context, which typically causes them to be interpreted in a radically different manner. A goal of many such rituals is to accomplish transcendence of the self – a blending into some larger reality. An obvious potential benefit is the fostering of social cohesion via the identification of a person as part of a larger group. So the feelings of awe, tranquillity, ecstasy, and belonging that someone might feel watching his country playing football or their favourite band are not unusual and similar processes operate in religious rituals, except they are interpreted in a different way, such as the closeness of God.

But elaborate ritual certainly isn't required to provoke a non-religious mystical experience. The Psychologist Abraham Maslow asked people to describe the "most wonderful experiences of their lives; happiest moments, ecstatic moments, moments of rapture…" He termed these moments "peak experiences" and found them to have a number of general characteristics.[24] These included "total attention on the object in question, complete absorption, disorientation in time and space, transcendence of the ego, and… fusion of the perceiver and the perceived' and 'wonder, awe… as before something great". These descriptions are similar to those reported by individuals claiming religious mystical experiences. Furthermore, Maslow reported that listening to music (particularly the classics) was one of the commonest ways people reported attaining peak experiences. These findings have since been backed up by several other studies which report that the same effects can be produced by "art, love, science, childbirth, creative work" and, no surprise, "religion".

What we learn from this type of research is that mystical experiences may stem from entirely natural processes, suggesting that in a sense the individuals reporting them are telling the "truth". That is, the experiences are real in a neurobiological sense, and when these individuals report having these sensations and feelings they are not lying.

But are they *actually* sensing God (or being filled with the Holy Spirit)? Some argue that nothing supernatural is being sensed and humans have developed the ability to have these experiences because they bestow some evolutionary advantage or are a by-product of our evolution.[25] Others reply that even though it is possible to describe what is happening in the brain during these experiences, they are still ultimately attributable to God, and rituals are merely the method of gaining access to God. Many researchers in this area are loath to extend their findings further, pointing out that "the external reality of religious precepts is neither confirmed nor disconfirmed by establishing brain correlates of religious experience". They warn it is not possible to say whether individuals having these experiences are actually sensing something truly "divine", and it is therefore possible that they really are sensing a higher being. Explaining the neurological events that create a visual experience of an object does of course not make the object somehow cease to exist and we might consider the same to be true of mystical experiences.

While this may be true, the fact remains that Charismatic Christian and, say, Buddhist explanations for the same neurobiological phenomena cannot both be true in general. As with evaluating the relative claims of religious texts, one is left searching for something uniquely persuasive, and research has persuasively shown that Holy Spirit manifestations lack it. On top of this, Alpha does not even attempt to address the question raised here. Instead, alternative explanations and rival claims are passed over in silence, as is typical of Gumbel. If the "leap of faith" is based on the phenomena discussed here it is a leap ultimately based, as with the "intellectual" element of Alpha Christianity, on an entirely credulous reading of the Bible.

Notes

1. Voskuil, P.H.A. (1983) The epilepsy of Fyodor Mikhailovitch Dostoevsky (1821-1881). *Epilepsia*, 24, 658-667
2. Waxman, S.G. (1975) The interictal behaviour syndrome of temporal lobe epilepsy. *Archives of General Psychiatry*, 32, 1580-1586
3. Dewhurst, K. & Beard, A.W. (1970). Sudden religious conversions in temporal lobe epilepsy. *British Journal of Psychiatry*, 117, 497-507
4. Azari, N.P., Nickel, J., Wunderlich, G., Niedeggen, M., Hefter, H., Tellmann, L., Herzog, H., Stoerig, P., Birnbacher, D., & Seitz R.J. (2001) Neural correlates of religious experience. *European Journal of Neuroscience*, 13, 1649-1652

5. McNamara, P. (2002) The motivational origins of religious practices. *Zygon*, 37 (1), 143-160

6. Muramoto, O. (2004) The role of the medial prefrontal cortex in human religious activity. *Medical Hyoptheses*, 62, 479-485

7. Ogata, A. & Miyakawa, T. (1998) Religious experiences in epileptic patients with a focus on ictus-related episodes. *Psychiatry and Clinical Neuroscience*, 52 (3), 321-325.

8. Field, H., & Waldfogel S. (1995). Severe ocular self-injury. *General Hospital Psychiatry*, 17:224–7.

9. Brown, A. (2006) Mother ruled insane in child deaths. *Globe and Mail* (Canada) 27th July.

10. D'Aquili, E. & Newberg, A.B. (1999) *The Mystical Mind: Probing the Biology of Religious Experience*. Fortress Press, Minneapolis.

11. Newberg, A., D'Aquili, E. & Rause, V. (2001) *Why God Won't Go Away*. Ballantine Books, New York.

12. Peters, K. (2001). Neurotheology and evolutionary theology: reflections on the mystical mind. *Zygon,* 36 (3), 493-500.

13. Spezio, M.L. (2001) Understanding biology in religious experience: the biogenetic structuralist approach of Eugene D'Aquili and Andrew Newberg. *Zygon*, 36 (3) 477-484.

14. Delio, I. (2003). Brain science and the biology of belief: a response. *Zygon*, 38 (3), 573-585.

15. Albright, C. R. (2001). Neuroscience in pursuit of the holy: mysticism, the brain and ultimate reality. *Zygon,* 36 (3), 485-492.

16. Newberg, A. (2001). Putting the mystical mind together. *Zygon*, 36 (3), 501-507.

17. Specifically, the autonomic nervous system which regulates basic bodily functions, such as heart rate, digestion and blood pressure. It is comprised of two usually antagonistic systems: the sympathetic (arousal) and parasympathetic (quiescent) systems. The sympathetic system causes a sense of arousal whereas the parasympathetic system maintains homeostasis and conserves the body's resources. These systems operate as part of the everyday functioning of a person in relation to the environment. For example, when a threat is detected the arousal system will activate to allow the body to expend the energy required to prepare the body for action and once the threat has disappeared it will defer to the quiescent system to slow breathing, etc to allow more efficient use of the body's energies.

18. That stimuli used in rituals can alter the autonomic nervous system is not in question. The best example is perhaps the physiological effects of music, with 120 years of experiments on the subject. For a review see: Juslin, P.N. & Sloboda, J.A. (2001) *Music and Emotion: Theory and Research*, Oxford University Press.

19. If an individual is pushed far enough into each state it can result in "spillover" resulting in activation of the other part of the ANS. For example, if a religious ritual pushed an individual so far into a hyperquiescent state then

eventually this would result in concurrent activation of the arousal system, resulting in very unusual sensations and perceptions. Unfortunately, a full explanation is not possible here.

20. This area they term the "orientation association area".

21. Gellhorn, E. & Kiely, W.F. (1972) Mystical states of consciousness: neurophysiological and clinical aspects. *Journal of Nervous and Mental Disease,* 154, 399-405.

22. This may also occur with concurrent involvement of the hypothalamus, which has an important role in producing pleasurable psychological states.

23. Norris, R.S. (2005). Examining the structure and role emotion: contributions of neurobiology to the study of embodied religious experience. *Zygon,* 40 (1), 181-199.

24. The following studies are cited in Gabrielson, A. (2001) Emotions in strong experiences with music In: *Music and Emotion: Theory and Research,* Oxford University Press.

25. For example, authors such as Richard Dawkins have advanced arguments as to why and how humans might have evolved to have these experiences and religion as a whole.

About the Authors

Stuart Abercrombie gained his PhD in chemistry from the University of Southampton and is pursuing an engineering career in California. Malcolm Hobbs gained his PhD in experimental psychology from the University of Southampton and currently works at a university in London.

Lightning Source UK Ltd.
Milton Keynes UK
19 November 2010

163162UK00003B/45/P